trust

trust

a godly woman's adornment

LYDIA BROWNBACK

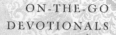 **CROSSWAY**

WHEATON, ILLINOIS

Library of Congress Cataloging-in-Publication Data
Brownback, Lydia, 1963–
   Trust : a godly woman's adornment / Lydia Brownback.
      p. cm. — (On-the-go devotionals ; #1)
   Includes bibliographical references.
   ISBN 978-1-58134-957-3 (tpb)
   1. Trust in God. 2. Christian women—Religious life. I. Title. II. Series.
BV4637.B825   2008
248.8'43—dc22   2007037924

Crossway is a publishing ministry of Good News Publishers.

VP		19	18	17	16	15	14	13	12	11
14	13	12	11	10	9	8	7	6	5	4	3

With gratitude to God
for Russ,
the rock of our family,
and
for Lisa,
who sacrifices much
for all of us

Contents

Introduction

Why Women Fear

*T*ornado rips through Kansas town . . . four dead in campus shooting . . . suicide bomber blows up school bus*—such news stories flash across the ticker tapes on our television screens. Day or night, we are bombarded with breaking news alerts of triple homicides, abused children, and the steady march toward moral collapse in Western civilization. And then there are the painful realities of our own lives—abandonment, disappointment, sickness, sorrow. Will the stream of death, loss, and destruction never end? The good news is that these heartbreaks will indeed cease. The end will come with the return of Jesus Christ. God has promised this, and he always fulfills his promises. In the meantime, all the horrors we witness on our television screens are not catching God off-guard. He has everything under the control of his mighty hand, which means that we have no reason to be afraid. So why do so many of us who profess to know Jesus Christ go about our lives in fear? Although God's Word tells us we have nothing to fear, the fact remains that many of us are afraid or anxious much of the time.

Do you struggle with fear? Have you felt its icy grip immobilizing your heart? Perhaps you aren't afraid exactly, but you are anxious. Stress is your constant companion, and you are nagged by worries over issues large and small. From restless thoughts to heart-racing panic attacks, we all struggle with fearful emotions to one degree or another, because fear is a fact in a fallen world. But according to Scripture, anxious fear doesn't have to be a fact for a daughter of God. In fact, the Bible tells us that there is no place for such fear for those who are in Christ Jesus. The Bible has a lot to teach us about what underlies our fears, and it also reveals the means to overcome them. I hope that as we look at God's Word together in this book, we will uncover great truths that will strengthen our faith and diminish our fears.

Overcoming anxiety begins with the realization that each one of our fears has a spiritual root. They are all directly linked to our view of God. It doesn't seem that way much of the time. Our overbooked agendas—even our preschoolers need scheduling calendars today—are natural stress generators. Most of us have too much to do with not enough time or money or energy to do it all, and trying to keep up brings stress to our marriages and worry lines to our faces. Nevertheless, our busy lives aren't the root cause of our anxiety. The root cause is our failure to understand who God is and how he is working in our lives. When we are rightly related to God, when we understand who he is—to and for us in Christ—we will realize we have no need to be anxious.

He is the God who numbers every hair on our heads (Matt. 10:30) and the one who has promised to supply all our needs (Phil. 4:19). He is the Father who gives us all things for our enjoyment (1 Tim. 6:17). He is the God who has promised to fulfill the heart desires of all who seek their happiness in him (Ps. 37:4). He is the one who tells us to be anxious for nothing and to cast all our anxieties on him because he cares for us (1 Pet. 5:7). He is the one who has already given us the best—his Son—and tells us that therefore we can certainly expect his intervention in all lesser things (Rom. 8:32).

If that is true, and it is because his Word says so, then why are we still fearful women? We are fearful because we don't really trust him. And we don't really trust him because at some level we don't really believe he is good. We simply don't take him at his word.

The only way we will learn to *trust* God is by getting to *know* God. When our understanding of him is deficient, we are going to view him wrongly. We are going to have a low view of him. If God is low in our estimation, then the things of this world are going to rate too high, which will snow us under. If we believe that somehow it is up to us to take control of our lives and the lives of those we love, fear is inevitable, because we simply aren't in control of anything. Many of us are quick to dismiss a link between our stress and our view of God. "I don't hold God in low regard," we object. "I live a Christian life and attend worship each Sunday, and I spend lots of time with other believers." But if we suffer from chronic anxiety and fear, we are kidding ourselves. Our view of God isn't as majestic as we think. A right view of God is the only thing that will dispel our illusion that we have to control our lives and that everything depends on us.

Additionally, our anxiety-producing, wrong view of God leads us to place too much value on the wrong things. If we don't know God very well, we can't see that he is the only thing ultimately worth living for, and we wind up living for ourselves instead. Our problems, our families—everything in our world—becomes supremely important. We put off the gentle and easy yoke of Christ that we are called to wear and instead attempt to harness God to a yoke of our own devising. Many of our anxieties and fears spring from dragging this self-made yoke. "The foolishness of a man twists his way, and his heart frets against the LORD" (Prov. 19:3 NKJV).

Some of us don't realize that we are trying to pull the wrong yoke. We reach toward dreams and goals designed to further God's kingdom and to bring blessing, and our prayer requests are for good things. But how do we react when things don't go according to plan? If, when our plans don't work out or our prayers aren't answered in the way or time we think best, we get frustrated and impatient and worried and fearful, that's a tip-off that something is off-kilter. All wrong views about God result in anxieties and fears about life. The health of our vertical relationship—our relationship with God—will always determine the health of our horizontal relationships—those we have with people, with life, and with ourselves. So the first thing to get straight is our view of God.

Since God overarches everything, we must view our lives and everything that happens to us through that lens. But we often don't. Instead we allow our circumstances to shape our view of God. We experience something bad, and we allow it to throw our belief about a loving, compassionate Father right out the window.

"Where is the God of all comfort in this heartache?"

"How could a powerful God let my baby die?"

"Why would a good God allow my marriage to fall apart?"

Sometimes when we cry out in our pain, asking God to make himself known, we can't find him. He seems faraway and distant, and we conclude that he just isn't as good and kind and powerful as we had thought. Our weak faith is shaken, and we wind up distancing ourselves from God, because our own means of comfort and the people who love us seem safer.

Perhaps the most faith-shaking, fear-generating experiences are those in which God provides a blessing and then seems to pull the rug out from under us by taking away the blessing as soon as we get a taste of it. The single woman who has waited years for a godly husband meets Mr. Right. God has provided at last! She feels God's smile as she prepares for her wedding and her new life as a married woman. And then two days before the wedding, Mr. Right changes his mind and calls the whole thing off. The grief-stricken bride wonders why God allowed her to get her hopes up, only to see them dashed to pieces. "Why would a loving God do that?" she asks, and her faith crumbles. God is not who she thought he was.

When we go through that sort of experience, our foundations can be shaken to the core. "I obviously cannot depend on God," we think, "so somehow I have to fix everything. And if God could do *this* to me, what other painful thing might he do?" What we don't see at such times and in the swirl of such thoughts is the fact that we were resting on the wrong foundation in the first place. Our view of God has actually been wrong all along. We thought we'd been relying on God, but the truth is, we'd actually been relying on our idea of God and on what we were hoping God would do for us to make our lives happier. What we don't see is that disappointments and other difficulties that seem to threaten our faith are really blessings in disguise. They are designed by

God to draw us closer to him, to enable us to see him as he really is, and to dispel our misconceptions about him and our wrong understanding of what it means to be a Christian.

When we first discover that God isn't who we'd thought, when he doesn't turn out to fit our image of him, our fall into doubt or unbelief can be extraordinary. "Who is God if he is not the one I can count on to rescue me from bad things?" we ask. "Is he a God I can be close to after all? I've always gone to him with everything large and small. Does he care? Or have I been kidding myself all this time?" When our view of a loving God is called into question, we don't know where to turn.

We don't realize during the throes of such an experience that he is, indeed, all those good things we'd believed before our fall into trouble. But how he works that goodness into our lives is often very different from what we expected—or wanted. Bad things happen to us because God is actually calling us into a deeper faith, one that trusts him and chooses to stay with him even when his love for us includes losses, the relinquishment of dreams and earthly hopes, and painful experiences for which there will be no remedy in this lifetime. Disappointments do not come from the hand of a cruel God; they come to us from the God who longs to relate and is actually drawing us nearer.

Times of intense disappointment and difficulty may well be indicators that God is drawing nearer to us, even though he may seem farther away. We find proof of this truth in Scripture, where we see several men and women who experienced great fear as a result of God's drawing near. The prophet Isaiah recounts his experience:

In the year that King Uzziah died I saw the Lord sitting upon a throne, high and lifted up; and the train of his robe filled the temple. Above him stood the seraphim. Each had six wings: with two he covered his face, and with two he covered his feet, and with two he flew. And one called to another and said:

"Holy, holy, holy is the LORD of hosts;
the whole earth is full of his glory!"

And the foundations of the thresholds shook at the voice of him who called, and the house was filled with smoke. And I said: "Woe is me! For I am lost; for I am a man of unclean lips, and I dwell in the midst of a people of unclean lips; for my eyes have seen the King, the LORD of hosts!" (6:1–5)

Isaiah saw God, but the vision certainly didn't evoke happy feelings. The experience caused him to cry out, "Woe is me!" What exactly made Isaiah afraid? He was fearful because his close view of God brought with it a realistic view of himself. John Calvin said that we can only know ourselves by first knowing God, and that is exactly what happened to Isaiah, who got a vivid glimpse of his sin, his "unclean lips." Isaiah was able to articulate what many of us cannot recognize in the midst of our fear—the instinctive response of sin coming face-to-face with holiness. Contrary to some popular teaching, we will be *more* aware of our sin, not *less*, as we get closer to God, and if we don't understand that this is what is happening, our anxiety and fear intensify.

Mary is another one to whom the Lord came near: "Now in the sixth month the angel Gabriel was sent by God to a city of Galilee named Nazareth, to a virgin betrothed to a man whose name was Joseph, of the house of David. The virgin's name was Mary. And having come in, the angel said to her,

'Rejoice, highly favored one, the Lord is with you; blessed are you among women!' But when she saw him, she was troubled at his saying, and considered what manner of greeting this was" (Luke 1:26–29 NKJV). The angel told her, "Do not be afraid, Mary, for you have found favor with God" (v. 30 NKJV). The angel came with good news, but Mary's initial response wasn't happiness; from what the angel said, it was fear. Don't we respond in the same way? God brings things into our lives—things meant to bless—and we shrink back when his coming shakes up our comfort zone and our carefully laid plans.

Then there was Moses. Consider what happened to him when he came upon the burning bush:

> *God called to him from the midst of the bush and said, "Moses, Moses! . . . Take your sandals off your feet, for the place where you stand is holy ground. . . . I am the God of your father—the God of Abraham, the God of Isaac, and the God of Jacob." And Moses hid his face, for he was afraid to look upon God. (Exod. 3:4–6 NKJV)*

The experiences of Isaiah, Mary, and Moses differed in the details, but the similarities in all three cases were the Lord's drawing near in a special way and the initial response of fear in each. From them we learn that sometimes God will come near to us in unexpected ways that disrupt our lives and make us afraid. In the cases of Isaiah, Mary, and Moses, the event was a prelude to a special work God had for each to do, but they didn't know that initially. All they knew was fear.

Those whom God calls to himself will likely experience such a divine intrusion at one time or another. And it is actually a gift. God is lowering the veil a bit so we can see the reality of who he is and who we are in relationship to him. Perhaps you are experiencing a divine intrusion in your life right now. If so, it just might be that God is preparing you for special work in his service.

One thing you can be sure of is that whatever plans God has in store for you, his drawing near is always designed to give you a deeper, heartfelt grasp of your need for Jesus. We often fail to understand who Jesus is for us now, today. Many of us see Jesus' role in our lives only in the past tense; he is the member of the Trinity who got us in the door of the Christian life through his death and resurrection two thousand years ago. But he is much more than that. It is because of his active work today, occurring moment by moment through our union with him, that we are enabled to live out the Christian life and to grow in our understanding of what that life is.

Do you realize that the only reason you experience God as your Father is because Jesus mediates that relationship every moment of every day? He didn't just get us in the door; he keeps us inside. Apart from him, we are too unrighteous to pray or to receive answers to our prayers or to have any favor with God whatsoever. None of us ever—at any time during any day of our lives—comes to God unaided by the present, active work of Christ. So when God comes near to us, even when it causes us fear, his primary purpose is to awaken us to the reality of the active, ongoing work of Christ.

When God comes near to us—and in our case, the method he uses is more likely to be a crisis, a loss, or an unmet need rather than a vision, an angel, or a burning bush—we are going to respond in one of two ways. Either we will cling to God in the midst of our fear, discovering in the process all that Jesus is for us, or we will run away from our only source of help. For those of us who struggle with chronic anxiety, with or without the experience of a spiritual crisis, it is because we have chosen the latter road. But God is still calling, still drawing near, and the discomfort of our anxiety is his merciful means to return us to the rest held out for us in Christ. May we find that rest together.

the
devotions

The Secret Places of the Heart

Do not be anxious about anything, but in everything
by prayer and supplication with thanksgiving
let your requests be made known to God.

PHILIPPIANS 4:6

*S*he's a Nervous Nellie," everyone says about Sara. That's because she tries to cope with daily stress by picking up the phone and venting her worries to whatever friend is available to listen. Sara worries about everything, from a broken dishwasher to a rainy forecast. But unlike Sara many of us keep our worries bottled up inside so that even those closest to us see nothing but a calm and steady exterior.

Maybe you have secret or hidden concerns that no one knows about, things you hesitate to tell even those closest to you. If you are a woman who struggles with overwhelming stress, yet you hide your anxiety from others, it is likely that you find yourself feeling isolated and lonely a good bit of the time. However, God knows all about your fears. He knows their underlying causes and the way you react to them. He also knows the way to get you past them.

God doesn't want you to be afraid; he wants to set you free. Fear, worry, and anxiety are not necessary for God's daughters. In fact, something we have forgotten in today's fast-paced lifestyle—or simply excused as unreasonable—is that anxiety is actually sin. But Paul's admonition is unconditional: "Do not be anxious about anything." He allows for no exceptions. Since God's Word says there is no reason to worry, that means there is no reason to worry. But we must choose to take him at his word and then apply the remedy that Paul gives here, which is prayer.

Is something weighing heavily upon you today? If so, whatever it may be, before you pick up the phone in search of consolation, take it to your Father in prayer. Tell him what you think you need and what you long for him to do, and then thank him for the way in which he will answer. He will indeed answer, and even before you see what he provides, if you are willing to let him decide the outcome, you will find the peace of knowing that your trouble is in his all-wise hands. Real faith—the kind that brings peace—is faith that lets God choose the best answer for you.

The *What-If* Woman

Trust in the LORD with all your heart,
and do not lean on your own understanding.

PROVERBS 3:5

*M*any of us are *what-if* women. What-if women spend a good deal of energy and time worrying not only about what might happen and about what they say and do, but also about what others think about what they say and do.

"What if I lose my job in the upcoming round of lay-offs?"

"What if I can't conceive?"

"What if that mole is cancerous?"

"I just can't get to the party next week. What if Sally never invites me again?"

Such worry about what may happen is fruitless. Think about it: our hovering over a situation cannot actually prevent the thing we are worried about from happening. The what-ifs can begin the moment we wake up and often last right on through the day. But God doesn't want us to be what-if women. What-iffing not only zaps our energy, it also indicates a lack of trust in God's wise and loving control over our affairs. He who cares to number every hair on our heads—something not even the vainest of us bothers to do—

cares much more about our trusting him with the upkeep of our homes, our health, our mobility, and our relationships with other people. Since he not only cares about these things but is also able to do something about them, he wants us to leave the ordering to him.

When we trust God to run our lives, we find that we are free to enjoy him and other people—free to live and love—because he is taking care of things. We are designed to glorify God and to enjoy him, not to spend our energies worrying about the details of daily life or fearing the pain of major crises. He will always supply what he knows we really need for every circumstance we face. Freedom from fear comes from believing that. It comes also from opening our hearts to embrace God's supply, even if his supply differs from what we think we need.

A Phobic's Only Remedy

"Fear not, for I am with you;
be not dismayed, for I am your God;
I will strengthen you, I will help you,
I will uphold you with my righteous right hand."

Isaiah 41:10

Traveling along the highway on her way into town one day, Katy was cut off suddenly by another driver, and she swerved into oncoming traffic, demolishing the family car. For months afterward, Katy felt heart palpitations and panic as soon as she approached an on-ramp. It became so bad that she began to make excuses to avoid going into town at all. Eventually she solved that problem by discovering alternate routes. Katy needs to hear the words of Isaiah the prophet: "Fear not, for I am with you; be not dismayed, for I am your God." The truth of Isaiah's utterance is the only remedy for women who suffer the debilitating effects of panic attacks. Maybe you are one of them.

The onset of what can become chronic panic attacks is often a solitary traumatic experience. Many of us can relate to what Katy deals with. Our trauma may, like Katy's, have occurred while driving; perhaps it was something completely different. Whatever the trauma, memory of the experience can take on monstrous proportions if we rehash it in our minds again and again. The fear takes on life-altering proportions, while cultivating within us an obsession with preventing its recurrence. If left to flourish, this obsession, like all obsessions, winds up ruling our lives, infringing on what we are willing to do and where we are willing to go. Anything that obsesses us, other than God, becomes our personal prison.

The beginning of such obsessions is often one defining incident, but it is enough to trigger an avalanche of fear. The only thing big enough to conquer this kind of fear is God, who rules every detail of every day of your life. Rest assured that nothing can touch you apart from your heavenly Father's permission. Out of his love for you, he is well able to prevent the thing you are so afraid of, and out of that same love he might allow it. Either way, whatever happens, he only allows what is going to work for your eternal happiness and blessing and his glory. Believe this, accept this, and you will find you can get back on the highway and out of your self-made prison cell. Exercise the faith you've been given, and you will know the truth: you are safe in God's keeping, every moment of every day.

God Knows Best

This God—his way is perfect;
the word of the LORD proves true;
he is a shield for all those who take refuge in him.

P s a l m   18 : 30

*B*ut I *have* prayed about it," Lory complained, "and I'm still struggling. I'm just afraid things will go wrong all the time—the house, the money, the kids—and I guess there's nothing I can do about it." The Bible tells us that we have no reason for anxiety and worry. So why are so many of us, like Lory, still fearful? Why can't we just banish the worry, anxiety, and bouts of panic? After all, none of us likes to feel afraid. The thoughts and sensations that signify and trigger fear are decidedly unpleasant, to say the least! The reason we can't just make it all go away is that fear isn't the root of our problem. Our anxiety is simply a symptom of something else, a tip-off that our hearts are bent in a wrong direction.

If we have asked God to deliver us from our fears, but we still aren't finding relief, it's not because God isn't answering. We are simply looking in the wrong place for the answer. God wants more than our symptom relief. He desires to get at the core of what underlies our fears, which, at the deepest level, have to do with our relationship with him. Fear is always a spiritual issue. For that reason we need to get beyond simply seeking to get rid of fearful feelings. When God allows the pain of fearful anxiety to linger in our hearts, it isn't because he delights to see us miserable—quite the contrary! But God allows us to experience fear at times to help us recognize our false foundations, things on which we are resting for security that have no more strength to support us than a mound of whipped cream.

Lory can't get past her fear because she is relying for safety on a smooth-running daily routine, which is, of course, not going to happen often. Are you anxious like Lory? If so, why not ask God to set you free from the underlying causes rather than simply removing your anxious feelings? He wants you to know that he is your rock—the only foundation that can bear the weight of your cares. He also wants to reprioritize the things about which you care. Much of Lory's anxiety comes from displaced priorities. She believes her greatest need is a hassle-free life. What she—and we—really need is the realization that our lives aren't all about now; our lives are preparation for an eternity of joy and pain-free living. We are going to be anxious if we make life all about the present, about what is only temporary and fleeting. God does care about our well-being, about the peace we experience in our daily lives, but never as an end in itself. He invites us to let him change our priorities and thereby to lead us out of anxiety and into peace.

The Goodness of God

The LORD is good to all,
and his mercy is over all that he has made.

PSALM 145:9

Kara wants to get married. In fact, she's been praying for a husband for over a decade now. All her friends are married; she is the only one from the old gang who is still single. Oh, Kara recognizes God's blessings in her life—great job, lots of friends, a good church—but she just can't get past the fear that her chances for having a family of her own are growing dimmer by the day. As a result, Kara isn't enjoying her single years, nor is she serving God with joy in her day-to-day work and in her interactions with others. But Kara's fear is not caused by her unmarried state. The reason Kara is anxious and unhappy is because she isn't trusting God in the area of her marital status. And the reason she isn't trusting him, although she doesn't recognize it, is because deep down in her heart she doesn't really believe God is being good to her by keeping her single.

Whether married or single, how many of us are just like Kara when it comes to trusting God with our deepest hopes? If we struggle to trust God, it's because at some level we don't really believe he is good. If you are trusting something besides

God to keep you safe and to make you happy, you are probably doubting God's goodness. Such doubts gain a foothold in our hearts when God doesn't act the way we think he should or the way we expect that he will.

But God often acts contrary to how we think a good God should act. The answer we think we need seems so logical and clear to our way of thinking, yet God does not provide it. That is where faith comes in. Real faith isn't the belief that God will do a particular thing; real faith is the conviction that God is good, no matter what he does and however he chooses to answer our prayers. God always has our best in mind, and he works to bring it about, no matter how it may look initially to our way of thinking.

You can trust him because he is good. And that goodness can be found—right now, today—in the very thing that you are so anxious about. Will you trust him? Will you believe he is being good to you? He is.

Safe and Secure

"All that the Father gives me will come to me, and whoever comes to me I will never cast out."

J O H N   6 : 3 7

*J*oanne's life gets more out of control by the day, but she can't go to God. She just knows he won't listen to her anymore. She's blown it too many times. "I promised God I'd never do it again—that I'd stop trying to crush out my stress with this sinful behavior. But I didn't keep my promise," she confessed to her pastor's wife. "Life just got too crazy, and I fell back into it. Now I'm more entrenched in it than ever before. What if God won't forgive me this time?"

Joanne is caught in sin, and because of it she fears that God is rejecting her. Are you afraid of doing something that might cause God to reject you? The Bible does tell us to fear God, but the sort of fear God wants from his daughters isn't terror. It's the sort of fear that hits us when we see Niagara Falls or a majestic sunset—an awestruck feeling mixed with wonder. That sort of fear, along with peace and joy, is what's available to us all the time when we come to God, if we come to him through Christ. Jesus gives us access to our heavenly Father; our "successful" performance does not.

If you are anxious about your acceptance with God, fly to

Jesus. He is your refuge. He is the way of access to God—no matter what you did yesterday, no matter what you are struggling with today. If you believe in your heart that Jesus paid in full for all your sins—past, present, and future—then you already have fellowship with a good Father.

If, on the other hand, you have not relinquished your heart to Jesus, if you are trying to make it to God on your own merits, then you have good reason to be afraid. That's because the only way to avoid God's rejection is by turning to Jesus. There is absolutely nothing you can do to please God or to earn his favor apart from Christ. But he is there for you if you will only turn to him. You never have to fear that he'll reject you if you come acknowledging your brokenness and your need for a savior. In fact, that is the only way you can come. No matter what you have done—a long time ago or within the past hour—Jesus will welcome you.

Building on Rock

*"Everyone who comes to me and hears my words
and does them, I will show you what he is like:
he is like a man building a house, who dug deep and laid
the foundation on the rock. And when a flood arose,
the stream broke against that house and could not
shake it, because it had been well built. But the one who
hears and does not do them is like a man who built
a house on the ground without a foundation.
When the stream broke against it, immediately it fell,
and the ruin of that house was great."*

LUKE 6:47–49

In this parable Jesus describes two types of people. The first person is someone strong, not easily shaken or fearful, because his dwelling is built on a rock-hard foundation. His dwelling is so firm that when the storms of life hit, he stays safe and unshaken inside. Jesus links this type of security to someone who hears his words and puts them into practice. The second person in the parable built a house with no foundation at all; so, of course, when the elements came against it, the house collapsed. Jesus likens this man to a person who hears his words but fails to live by them.

Which of the two people in Jesus' parable best describes you? Your stress level is one way to know. If you are living under the weight of constant tension, if you feel a compulsive need to control your surroundings, it is likely because you are attempting to build on something apart from Christ. We are prone to do this even after giving our lives to him. As long as we live, we are going to be tempted to build our security on our possessions or on people, but we don't see this because we aren't thinking in terms of Jesus *or* my husband, Jesus *or* my house, Jesus *or* my career. Instead we are operating under Jesus *and* my husband, Jesus *and* my house, Jesus *and* my career.

But we can't have it both ways. We are either resting on Jesus or we are resting on a Jesus substitute. The security for which we long will never be found in Jesus *and* something or someone else; it will be found in him alone. Every Jesus substitute or supplement will eventually collapse beneath us. God will see to that. He is faithful to us, and he will ensure that anything on which we rest apart from Christ won't give us the illusion of security indefinitely. If you are anxious and afraid, could it be that God is in the very process of pulling your substitute or supplement out from under you? If so, he isn't doing this to be unkind to you; he is doing it to show you where your security really lies.

Are you willing to rest on a single foundation? Jesus plus something else does not double your security. It actually takes it away. The only security is Jesus plus nothing.

False Security

"Fear not, nor be afraid;
have I not told you from of old and declared it?
And you are my witnesses!
Is there a God besides me?
There is no Rock; I know not any."

Isaiah 44:8

It could all be nothing more than gossip," Caroline reassures herself. But it's hard to dismiss the concern when the source is so reliable. Rumors have been circulating for weeks about a company-wide layoff, one that will surely include her husband if it happens. Caroline and her husband have always been grateful to God for his abundant provision. But now, faced with a pending layoff, Caroline wonders, "How will we afford the mortgage payments and the kids' tuition? Our whole lifestyle will change!" She has become devastated by moment-by-moment, peace-killing dread.

Caroline's exorbitant fear in the face of her husband's job loss reveals that she has been depending more on God's provision than on God himself. Are we like Caroline? Just because we assent to the truth that God is our rock does not mean we fully believe that truth. Sometimes the only way we can tell is how we react when life falls apart. When our paychecks cease, when our health declines, or when a loved one leaves us, then we will know what our real rock is. If it isn't God himself, we are likely to feel just as Caroline does, because the thing on which we have been relying for safety is no longer providing the protection we have come to expect from it.

What is your rock—not the one you say is your rock, but the one you actually lean on? One way to know is to examine whatever has the power to make you anxious. What comes to mind just before you feel afraid? What circumstances are you facing today, or might have to face tomorrow, that overwhelm you with faith-quenching anxiety? On whom or what do you depend to get you through the day? "Whatever assumes in our lives a practical importance that is greater than God will *become god* to us. And since we become what we worship, to let an unanswerable problem *become god* to us is the surest way to guarantee that life will be characterized at its heart by defeat."[1]

Whatever that is in your life—a thing or idea or person or place—is sooner or later going to crumble. Jesus is the only rock that won't ever break, and those who lean on him find God to be all they need.

---

[1] Os Guinness, *God in the Dark: The Assurance of Faith Beyond a Shadow of a Doubt* (Wheaton, IL: Crossway Books, 1996), 152, emphasis in the original.

People Pleasers

"I, I am he who comforts you;
who are you that you are afraid of man who dies,
of the son of man who is made like grass,
and have forgotten the LORD, your Maker,
who stretched out the heavens
and laid the foundations of the earth,
and you fear continually all the day
because of the wrath of the oppressor,
when he sets himself to destroy?
And where is the wrath of the oppressor?"

ISAIAH 51:12–13

We women tend to wrap a good bit of our lives around our relationships, don't we? We want to be liked and loved and to gain the approval of those around us. But when this natural desire becomes a basis for our well-being, then we can expect a good bit of turmoil and anxiety. Using others to build ourselves up, to fulfill us, and to meet our needs just won't work. Sooner or later, because people are sinners, they are going to let us down.

Are you tempted to seek security in your relationships? If

you feel that your survival depends on the love and approval of a spouse, a friend, a family member, your employer, or a neighbor, then your personal security system is faulty. Consider your motivations in showing love to others. If you detect an underlying compulsion to obtain a compliment or word of approval, it's a pretty sure bet that you have placed your well-being in their hands.

Desiring the love and approval of the significant people in our lives is natural; however, if we feel that we must have that to be happy, then a good desire has become a destructive one. We are attributing to people what rightfully belongs to God, which is why we are never able to live at rest with ourselves and at peace with others. Relational security that displaces security in God is a guaranteed anxiety generator because we will never find from people all we are looking for. Do you see yourself here? If so, don't be discouraged. View it instead as an opportunity. Realizing that you cannot obtain your desires from the people in your life is a catalyst to look elsewhere, to God, where you will find what you've been seeking all along.

Fear of Man

*The fear of man lays a snare,
but whoever trusts in the LORD is safe.*

PROVERBS 29:25

*M*elanie has been stuck in a dead-end relationship for over five years. Her friends just don't understand it. Why would a together girl such as Melanie stay with a man like Jake? Jake can't keep a job—he's cycled through three jobs during the past two years. His church attendance is spotty, and he often teases Melanie in a mean way in front of other people. "But I really love him," Melanie protests. "I want to marry him, and if I can just keep motivating him in his career and in his walk with God, I think we'll have a good marriage. He says he just can't do it without me, and he told me that if I just cut back on my ministry activities, I'll have more time to help him get his act together." Melanie's friends feel sorry for her. But actually Melanie *is* getting something from the relationship—a sense of security. As long as Melanie can make Jake dependent on her, the chances that he will abandon her are slim.

Psychologists use the label *codependency* for such relationships; the biblical term is idolatry. Relational idolatry breeds anxiety. Yet many women get caught in it and can't seem to break away even when they determine to do so. They remain stuck in such relationships because they are trying to free themselves from the wrong thing. But Jake is not the one Melanie is idolizing; she is actually idolizing herself. When we cling to ungodly entanglements in order to gain something for ourselves—even something good like love or security or acceptance—we are, at the core, committing an act of self-worship. It's worship turned inward rather than upward, which is the very definition of idolatry, and it is always the pathway to a stressful life.

One of the ways we can tell if we are basing our security on the acceptance of others is the way we react to people. Do we feel anxious after spending time with them, mentally reworking the things we've said, obsessing over our words and wishing we'd phrased things differently? If so, is it because we are worried about how our words reflect on God and on the feelings of others, or are we fretting over how our words reflect on ourselves? Are we concerned that our words may have hurt someone, or are we fearful that we have said or done something of which others might not approve? If our peace of mind is dependent on always saying the "right" thing in order to keep people pleased with us, of course we will feel anxious!

The cure for our people fears is to love people more and to need them less. Once we begin to move in a God-centered, others-oriented direction, which may at times entail separating from a relationship if it is an unbiblical one, we will experience freedom and a peace that will never be possible otherwise.

Resting on Self-Righteousness

For by works of the law no human being will be justified in his sight, since through the law comes knowledge of sin.

ROMANS 3:20

*G*od is not a mean tyrant, but some of us see him in just that way—hard to please, tapping his celestial finger in impatience with our imperfections, and willing to hand out blessings only when we've arrived at certain spiritual heights. Nowhere in Scripture do we find such ideas about God. But that is the image we are going to wind up with if we try to win God's approval by what we do and say. Surely we want God's acceptance, but we just aren't up to obtaining it. Seeking the blessings of salvation by self-effort will get us no farther than walking on a treadmill. We will find ourselves living under an ever-thickening cloud of fear, because nothing we do can make us right with God. Only Christ can do that.

Perhaps you have taken Jesus as your Savior, but you are still lacking assurance that God accepts you. No matter what you do, you can't grasp the idea of a kind, loving Father who longs to relate. If so, what have you been doing about that? Perhaps you have doubled your efforts for God—more serving, better attitudes—in an attempt to secure the divine favor that you seem to be missing. If this is your default in your dealings with God, chances are good that, instead of the love and joy you long for, God seems more remote than ever.

There is only one way out of the tangle, and that is to stop your efforts. Stopping feels counterintuitive, but it's actually the only way you'll find restful assurance that God accepts you. When you stop trying to get yourself right with God and instead simply rest in Jesus, you'll see that God doesn't go away. You will be surprised to discover that your efforts to clean up for him were actually contributing to your sense of distance from God. The only way to get near him, the only way to know him as Father and Friend, is to forsake yourself and rest in Christ. "Draw near to God, and he will draw near to you," "wrote the apostle James (James 4:8), and the only way to do so is by looking at Christ.

We believe in our hearts and declare with our lips that Jesus is the only way—we believe it, but often we don't live it. If we profess Christ and sing his praises, yet we aren't enjoying the peace that comes through him, let's see whether there is a performance treadmill under our feet and make a decision to step off. By uniting us to Christ, God has set us free from bondage, and our liberty is there for the taking.

No Ifs

For all have sinned and fall short of the glory of God,
and are justified by his grace as a gift,
through the redemption that is in Christ Jesus.

R O M A N S   3 : 2 3 - 2 4

*W*hat is the basis for our security with God? How do we
know that he listens to our prayers and forgives our sins and
takes care of us each day? Many of us are anxious about that:

> "I made a terrible mistake years ago by marrying an unbeliever.
> How can I expect God to help me now? I am to blame for the
> mess I've made, and I just have to figure out how to live with
> it."

> "I am so overwhelmed by this project, and my boss is skeptical
> that I can make the deadline. I know God is there to help me, but
> I missed my quiet time today, so I took myself away from his help.
> It's up to me now."

> "I just can't conquer my sin of overeating. I'm doing okay, and
> then I have a really bad day, and my resistance just goes right out
> the window. I just know God won't listen to me about anything
> until I've mastered this."

We get fearful and anxious because our default thought
pattern is that God will do his part *if* we do ours. The reality

is, however, that there is no *if*. God has already done his part by sending his Son, and in so doing he completed forever our eternal security and adoption into his family. God hates our attempts to earn his favor, not only because they deny the finished work of Jesus, but also because those attempts keep us from enjoying his fellowship.

Attempting to earn God's favor will always lead to weariness in the Christian life, or to fear, because no matter what we do, we will never measure up. Nothing we do is up to God's standards. That's why Christ not only died for us—he lived a perfect life for us as well. Do you know what that means? It means that when we fail to measure up, God looks at how Jesus measured up, and he applies that to us. It means that God exchanges the perfect choices Jesus made in his earthly relationships for our bad choices. The intimate fellowship Jesus had with the Father while he walked this earth is exchanged for our halfhearted quiet times. It means that Jesus' resistance to temptation covers our failures to resist. There are no ifs; Jesus took care of all that.

Self-Salvation?

Behold, his soul is puffed up; it is not upright within him,
but the righteous shall live by his faith.

HABAKKUK 2:4

I've been unemployed for two months now," Lynn told her friend. "I can't figure out what God wants from me before he'll provide me with work. I've turned away from every possible sin I can think of, but maybe there's one I can't put my finger on. Maybe God is waiting for me to figure that out before he gives me a new job. I just wish I knew what more he wants."

Do you think like Lynn? Perhaps right now life is not going the way you'd hoped, and you fear it's because you are doing something wrong, or that more God wants more from you than you are giving and doing. You think that if you could just figure out what more God expects from you, then your life would begin to go in the direction you want. But the Bible makes clear what God wants from us. It boils down to one primary thing—to trust in what Christ did on our behalf.

But even though the Bible makes this plain, we feel compelled to earn his favor by our good works and words. What drives us to ignore the simple truth of Scripture is a desire to be in control of our lives. There is something we want or need in a particular way and time, and we think we stand a better chance of getting God to accommodate our way if we bring something extra to the table in our dealings with him. If we are wrestling along these lines, we ought to consider the possibility that hidden within our hearts somewhere is the desire to manage God. Anxiety is an indicator. Whenever we attempt to do something impossible—and managing God is indeed impossible—anxiety is going to be right there.

He knows our situation inside and out. He is totally in control of our employment status, our marital status, our finances, our friendships, and our health. And his control is governed by his kindness and love. Since this is the God to whom we belong and for whom we live, we can leave the ordering of our lives completely in his hands. He will never arrive too late. God doesn't want our efforts at self-improvement. He wants our trust in his kindness toward us in Christ.

Nothing More Than Feelings

But some of them said, "Could not he who opened the eyes of the blind man also have kept this man from dying?"

*B*ut God wouldn't want you to be unhappy," Christine protested when Amy shared with her how depressed she'd been feeling for the past several weeks. "So what if you go into debt taking that cruise?" Christine added. "God would want you to do whatever it takes to feel better."

Christine means well, and she certainly has captured a small bit of truth: God takes no pleasure in our pain. "He does not willingly afflict or grieve the children of men" (Lam. 3:33). But Christine has twisted this truth into an untruth. God does allow pain. In fact, there will be times when he leads us straight into it, even when it pains him to do so. Jesus could have spared Mary and Martha the pain of Lazarus's death, but he did not, even though that death caused him to weep over the sisters' grief at the loss of their brother. This seems to make no sense; why wouldn't Jesus simply have spared them all the trouble? Jesus didn't spare them because he knew that the pain was a prelude to great blessing, a blessing the sisters would have missed if Jesus had brought it along earlier. You can read the entire story and discover the blessing that came about in John 11.

Mary and Martha questioned, "Why, Lord, did this happen when you could have stopped it?" And Jesus' answer to the sisters is his answer to us as well: "Did I not say to you that if you would believe you would see the glory of God?" But we don't think in his terms much of the time. We care much less about long-term results and the glory of God than we do about simply feeling better. If we feel blue for more than a day or two, we mentally take stock of what we can change in order to fix how we feel. Sometimes, certainly, feelings are a good indicator of a need for change, but when changing can only be brought about by ungodly or questionable means, it is a call to leave things as they are for the time being.

During difficult times we don't have to let our downcast feelings rule our lives. If we lay hold of the truth about God—that he is up to something good in our trouble—then we won't be afraid of how we feel. God wants us to enjoy the peace that comes from a mind set on him and on his purposes rather than on how we feel. A Christ-focused life is a stable life, because the joy that comes along with it doesn't hinge, as do our human emotions, on daily ups and downs.

Afraid of the Pain

More than that, we rejoice in our sufferings,
knowing that suffering produces endurance, and
endurance produces character, and character produces hope,
and hope does not put us to shame, because God's love
has been poured into our hearts through the Holy Spirit
who has been given to us.

ROMANS 5:3–5

*I*sn't it true that most of us worry less about what's happening in our lives than about what *might* happen? We are unnerved at the prospect of an illness, a loss, a financial setback. What is it we're so afraid of, exactly? We can begin by considering our particular fears, asking, "What is the worst thing that could happen to me if this actually comes to pass?" By engaging in such consideration, we can usually get to the bottom of our worry: "I'll be broke" or "I'll end up alone" or "I'll be in physical pain." Once we've identified what's making us afraid, we can ask the question again: "What's the worst thing that will happen if I end up broke or alone or in physical pain?" And then we get to the heart of our fear: "I'll suffer."

None of us wants to suffer, certainly, but sooner or later

we all do. We might as well face it. But we don't have to dread suffering because God has good purposes for our pain. And he sets the limits on our individual trials too, allowing only what is absolutely necessary to prepare us to desire and to enjoy the life he has in mind for us. But the fact that our dread of disaster pulses in our hearts indicates how little we really want the life God has for us if that life includes suffering.

Living in our particular society, a determined resistance to pain seems only right and normal. In our culture, where happiness and personal rights are the supreme good, anything that makes us feel unhappy is diagnosed as the supreme bad. We adopt the thinking of society and wind up confusing the principle of democracy—life, liberty, and the pursuit of happiness—with the principles of the Bible, which teach that suffering is not our enemy but a friend in disguise.

Because God loves us, he will visit us with this friend as need be. But we do not have to live in fear of it, because all our suffering is controlled by a God who loves us. "Therefore let those who suffer according to God's will entrust their souls to a faithful Creator while doing good" (1 Pet. 4:19). The God who loves us sets limits around whatever might affect us, and all that he allows is designed to shape us for life in his kingdom—now and for eternity. If we choose to understand and to accept that this is the purpose behind all we suffer, we will stop being afraid of dark days.

Feelings and Fear

Whoever confesses that Jesus is the Son of God,
God abides in him, and he in God.

1 John 4:15

Fear and feelings-oriented living go hand in hand. That is because feelings are as unpredictable, as unstable, as wind. Just as wind does not exist outside of the natural forces that generate it into a calm breeze or the frenzy of a hurricane, feelings are purely responses—sometimes good responses and sometimes bad ones—to the ups and downs that God brings into our lives. Unpredictable and unstable as they are, if we allow our feelings to determine our well-being, rather than allowing our standing in Christ to determine our feelings, we are going to be anxious about everything all of the time.

Nowhere is this more applicable than in our relationship with God. Joy and peace are characteristic of the Christian life, but inevitably there will be times, whether through sin or through some hardship or through just being human, when joy and peace elude us. But the presence or absence of good feelings is no measure of God's favor. Christ is the only measure. If we look to our feelings as a barometer of how well we are doing with God, using them to measure whether he is pleased with us, then our faith will be shaken during times when feelings of joy and peace are hard to come by.

How wonderfully freeing it is to flip-flop our feelings with faith—and we can do it because it is God's will that we do so. Our relationship with God and all the good that accompanies it are secure in Christ, no matter how we feel. Christ is all we need for an accurate assessment of where we stand with God. He is the means of our salvation—from beginning to end. During times when God's presence cannot be felt, when the joy that is meant to accompany our Christian walk has left us, we can remember his promise: "I will never leave you nor forsake you" (Heb. 13:5).

Eyes Wide Open

It is in vain that you rise up early
and go late to rest,
eating the bread of anxious toil;
for he gives to his beloved sleep.

P SALM 127:2

*M*any of us find ourselves wide awake and worried in the middle of the night, unable to sleep because anxious thoughts of the day gone by or of the day lying ahead have hooked our minds. We mull over a situation to the point where we blow it all out of proportion, and it is not until morning that we pause to ask ourselves what all the anxious fuss was about. Troubles are magnified in the middle of the night.

If we tend to worry most often between midnight and dawn, could there be a link between our middle-of-the-night fretting and the fact that this is the time when we have least control over our lives? Let's consider the possibility that our problems seem less overwhelming in the morning because we are under the illusion that we can get up out of bed and regain control. Elisabeth Elliot wrote, "I sometimes find myself turning something over and over mentally in the early hours of the morning, long before my alarm clock beeps. That is a bad time to indulge in thinking, first, because it is the time for sleeping and, second, because there is nothing I can do about whatever it is at that hour anyway."[1]

The ability to sleep, or the lack thereof, is more often than not a spiritual issue. That is certainly true when what is keeping us awake is worry, something God has told us not to do. Our minds recycle the events and conversations of the day gone by, and we obsess over what we should have done or said differently, rather than placing the matter in God's hands. Sleep will come much more easily to many of us if, when we are assailed with middle-of-the-night anxieties, we will simply pray, "Lord, I think I made a mess of things. So I am placing the whole situation in your hands. Do with it what you will." Our pre-dawn prayers usually include just the first of those sentences. But sleep will come if we pray all of that and really mean it.

---

[1] Elisabeth Elliot, *Discipline: The Glad Surrender* (Grand Rapids, MI: Revell, 1994), 61.

Control Freaks

The LORD visited Sarah as he had said,
and the LORD did to Sarah as he had promised.

GENESIS 21:1

*S*arah and Abraham had been waiting a long time for a baby. In fact, God had promised them a child. But that was ages ago, and no baby had come. Had they misunderstood God? Maybe they'd read too much into his promise. So the couple gave a good, hard look at the facts confronting them and took matters into their own hands. At Sarah's instigation, Abraham fathered a child through his wife's maid, Hagar—a son whom Sarah claimed legally as her own child. Although such surrogacy was common practice in ancient Israel, God had made clear that the promised child would come directly from their marital union, which is why the solution they devised created more problems than it solved. Strife and tension filled the patriarchal household for a long time afterward (Gen. 15–16, 21).

We so easily adopt the mind-set of Sarah and Abraham when God's promises are slow in coming. Sometimes we stop believing that God will keep his promises; other times we attempt to reinterpret his promises to suit our plans and our schedule. If we stop trusting that God is able to act or to make clear to us how we are to act, then we are certain to seek our own solutions by laying hold of what lies right at hand. The bottom line is that we hate to wait. We crave a life we can control, and if we give into this craving, we are going to be tempted to wrest our circumstances away from God when he doesn't act as we think he should.

If God hasn't yet worked out a troubling situation in your life, attempting a solution of your own devising will lead only to more anxiety, just as it did for Sarah and Abraham. Despite their sinful control-taking, God visited them afterward and reminded them of his promise. He hadn't changed his mind, even though they had sought their blessing in another direction. But Sarah and Abraham, caught up in the throes of their troublesome, self-made solution—the child Ishmael—weren't as open to the really good blessing God had in store. That's why, when God came to remind them about the child of promise, Abraham begged, "Let it be Ishmael" (Gen. 17:18).

Just so, our self-made solutions will distract us from keeping our eye out for God's promises. We'll be like Abraham, begging for second best when the ultimate blessing awaits us. Perhaps you have awakened to the fact that you've already done this, and you are caught in the tangle of a bad decision. But just as God didn't take back his promise to Abraham, he won't take away his promises to you either; so you need not fear that you've missed your chance. Turn back to God, and wait for him anew. He always keeps his promises. J. I. Packer wrote:

> If I found I had driven into a bog, I should know that I had missed the road. But this knowledge would not be of much comfort if I

then had to stand helpless watching the car sink and vanish: the damage would be done, and that would be that. Is it the same when a Christian wakes up to the fact that he has missed God's guidance and taken the wrong way? Is the damage irrevocable? Must he now be put off course for life? Thank God, no. Our God is a God who not merely restores, but takes up our mistakes and follies into his plan for us and brings good out of them. This is part of the wonder of his gracious sovereignty. "I will restore to you the years that the locust has eaten . . . and ye shall eat in plenty, and be satisfied, and praise the name of the Lord your God, that hath dealt wondrously with you" (Joel 2:25f).[1]

---

[1] J. I. Packer, *Knowing God* (Downers Grove, IL: InterVarsity Press, 1973), 219.

Fretful Living

Be still before the LORD and wait patiently for him;
fret not yourself over the one who prospers in his way,
over the man who carries out evil devices!
Refrain from anger, and forsake wrath!
Fret not yourself; it tends only to evil.

PSALM 37:7-8

I don't think you should go ahead with this," Diane's mother advised her. "This condo far exceeds your budget, and I think you are going to wind up in financial trouble if you purchase it."

"Mom, it must be the one God has for me. I've been praying for the right place for months now, and it's the only one to come along that I really like."

"Well, doesn't the Bible instruct us to be wise in money matters? Also, it's so far away from your job and your church. I think you are going to feel isolated living way out there."

"God will work all that out. I just better move on this or I'll miss my chance."

How do you deal with waiting? Most of us look to see what steps we can take to relieve the anxious tension. We are tempted to control our lives however we can. Quick and active problem-solving is sometimes the good and right thing to do, but when our efforts create more trouble or bring deeper distress, it is worth considering the possibility that we are trying to solve our difficulties independently of God. And if our solutions violate biblical principles, we can be sure we are going in the wrong direction. Do our attempts at an immediate solution mask an unwillingness to wait for God and to live by his timetable? When life is difficult, when we or someone we love is in distress, do we attempt to force God's promises to come true in our own way and time?

Psalm 37 cautions us not to fret because fretting causes only harm. Fretting is anxious hovering, a sinful wresting of control from God; it's complaining with an impatient spirit. Fretting adds fuel to the fire of our difficulties, and if we indulge in it, it won't be long before we find ourselves elevating our weak and inadequate reason above God and his Word. Once this happens, life begins to look like a complicated jigsaw puzzle where fitting all the pieces together is all up to us.

Have you prayed about your trouble? Real prayer includes letting go of your insistence on a particular answer or timing. If you have really prayed, you can simply rest and wait for God. Trust him with your concern, and your anxiety will clear away.

Mistaken Identity

*Beloved, we are God's children now, and what we will be
has not yet appeared; but we know that when he appears
we shall be like him, because we shall see him as he is.*

1 JOHN 3:2

*W*hen we are introduced to people, we're asked, "So, what do you do?" And we typically have a good bit of our identity wrapped up in the answer we give. All too often we mistake what we *do* for who we *are*. Some of us want an identity that we don't have. Single women want to be defined as wives. It's hard to be single when so many others around us have been chosen by a man to bear his name and his children and to have the identity of Mrs. So-and-So. Likewise, married women usually want the identity of mother, and career women desire the identity afforded by a particular title on their business card.

But our calling is not our identity. If we want to be known as a corporate director, we won't be content as a manager. If we seek to build our identity on being a wife, we won't be content being single. If we define ourselves by motherhood, we may become fearful about our purpose in life when we don't have children, or when the children we do have grow up and leave home. Mothers who build their identity on mothering are sometimes tempted to keep on bearing children solely because this is the only thing they can envision doing. But look at how the apostle Paul defined himself: "For me to live is Christ" (Phil. 1:21). Christ was Paul's whole reason for living, his entire identity.

Wife, mother, CEO—these are hats we wear and things we do; they are not who we are. Our only lasting identity is Jesus Christ, and if we seek identity elsewhere, we will never be satisfied, since nothing else has the ability to define us indefinitely. Let's define ourselves by Jesus. He is our identity more than any husband, child, or job.

Getting Unstuck

*So we see that they were unable to enter
because of unbelief.*

HEBREWS 3:19

*E*lena is perplexed. After a productive meeting with a financial counselor, she is still struggling with intense bouts of panic about her finances. The counselor had been encouraging, advising Elena that she's on the right track in terms of savings and budgeting. She's in good financial shape. But Elena can't shake the dreaded feeling that comes when she opens a bill or the fear that assails her when the engine light on the dashboard begins flashing the "service needed" warning. "How much will this cost me?" she frets.

Sometimes, after doing all we can to address our fear, we can't seem to get out from under it. We feel stuck. Perhaps you are stuck. You yearn for peace and rest, but your anxious thoughts reach out and ensnare you again and again. Why does this happen? Sometimes we stay stuck because the thing we have identified as the cause of our fear is not really the root of our problem. In Elena's case, feeling good about her financial picture isn't really what she needs, which is why the financial counseling didn't alleviate her stress. Elena's real need is to find her sufficiency in God, no matter her financial status. Elena has been trying to solve a money problem when her primary issue is a belief problem.

The same is true for all of us, no matter what earthly care grips us with fear. The underlying source of our anxiety—most, if not all, of it—is unbelief in God and a corresponding unwillingness to follow him. That's what the author of Hebrews was getting at in his letter. The Old Testament Israelites, about whom he was writing, had God's presence to guide them by day and by night; they had all the food they could possibly need miraculously provided in the manna that God rained down from heaven, and they had the guarantee of God's protection. Despite all this—God's presence, provision, protection, and promises—the Israelites were constantly fearful about what might go wrong. As a result they were unable to find the heart rest that was available to them every moment. The author of Hebrews didn't think it necessary to point out how hard it was for the Israelites to cope with life in the wilderness; instead he laid the source of their inability to enjoy peace squarely on their unbelieving hearts.

If we would only believe that what is right here for us—life with the God who protects and provides—is sufficient, we would quickly discover that we have no need to seek our fulfillment anywhere else.

Whose Fault Is Our Fear?

Take care, brothers, lest there be in any of you an evil,
unbelieving heart, leading you to fall away from
the living God. But exhort one another every day,
as long as it is called "today," that none of you may be
hardened by the deceitfulness of sin.

HEBREWS 3:12–13

I'm always waiting for the lightning to strike,"
said my backslidden friend only half jokingly. "In
this long season away from God, I've indulged in
a lot of sexual sin, and I've experienced no consequences—no STDs or stuff like that." My friend didn't
realize that he was already in the grip of the worst possible
consequence—an increasing appetite for those sins and a corresponding callousness toward God.

The same callousness happens when we continue to
indulge in anxiety, which always springs from the belief that
God isn't able to care for us properly or that what he provides
isn't enough for us. Such a belief is really unbelief, and the
longer we live in it, the harder our hearts become to the truth
of God's goodness, kindness, love, and desire to abundantly
provide. What are we to do if we detect hardness in our

hearts? We acknowledge the truth to ourselves and to God by rightly identifying our anxiety as sin. We give our anxiety its proper name—unbelief. If we are living in fear, there is unbelief in our hearts. Unbelief underscores every fear and every act of sin we commit. Unbelief is the assertion in our hearts, even if it doesn't appear to be so, that God cannot be trusted.

We think that our fears are caused by our circumstances, but that just isn't true. Unbelief is the source of all our fears, because unbelief, taking up residence in our minds and hearts, casts dispersion on the good character of God. When we doubt God's kind intentions, we will certainly go astray in our hearts and eventually become hardened to the comfort he would bring us. The letter of Hebrews wasn't written to unbelievers; it was written to Christians, which shows us that being numbered among God's people doesn't exempt us from the danger of hardening our hearts. But a hard heart is not the end of the story. We can turn away from the lie of unbelief right now and put our faith in our good Father.

The Truth about Pride

Pride goes before destruction,
and a haughty spirit before a fall.

PROVERBS 16:18

I don't believe in God," Brittney said to Erica, "and I don't understand why you do either. I mean, what's he done to prove to you that he's there? You're so miserable all the time, depressed and afraid of your own shadow."

Both Brittney and Erica are living in unbelief, even though one of them, Erica, is a Christian. Brittney refuses to believe in the existence of God, whereas Erica refuses to believe in the goodness of God. Unbelief is leaning on our interpretation of life instead of on God's character and his Word. Anyone can be unbelieving, Christian or not, because the root of unbelief is pride, and pride lurks in every human heart. Unbelief and pride are flipsides of the same coin, and they fight to take up residence in our hearts, leading us to think we can manage the world and our own affairs better than anyone else, including God.

We shudder when we hear about murders and rapes and child abuse—horrible sins—but the truth is that pride is even worse. Pride was the sin that brought down Satan (Isa. 14:12–15). Pride brings down kingdoms, marriages, and individuals. Pride seeks to displace God and raise ourselves into his rightful place over us. Pride is often the hardest sin to deal with because we are oblivious to the choke hold it has on our hearts.

Pride is often hard to detect, but we can be sure it is there whenever we are anxious, worried, or fearful about our circumstances. We can be sure it is there when we are miserable without something we want or think we need. We can be sure it is there if we resist God's way when it contradicts our idea of what is fair. If we really believe that God is who he says he is, our lives will be characterized by peace rather than by turmoil. We will find rest in depending on him rather than stress from relying on ourselves. How do we get there? The Bible tells us how. By pursuing humility. "Humble yourselves, therefore, under the mighty hand of God," writes Peter, "so that at the proper time he may exalt you, casting all your anxieties on him, because he cares for you" (1 Pet. 5:6–7).

The Blessings of Humility

For the LORD takes pleasure in his people;
he adorns the humble with salvation.

PSALM 149:4

Humility is God's will for each of his daughters. In fact, God wants humility for us more than he wants our service or our good works, because humility honors our good God and enables us to live confidently with peace, contentment, and joy. Humility is the seed that flowers into real trust that God knows what he is doing. A humble woman will gladly let God run the show, even when his leading seems to contradict her own logic.

God will go to great lengths to humble us so that we don't miss out on his blessings. How does God produce humility in our hearts? He often does so by bringing into our lives wildernesses, weaknesses, and trials of all sorts. It is in times of trouble, times when our personal resources run dry, that we are most likely to look for evidence of God's goodness and power at work. He sends wildernesses and trials into our lives to teach us to depend solely on him. However, we may fail to benefit from these difficulties if we respond wrongly.

Wayne Mack writes, "God uses difficult times in our lives to teach us that there is only one reason that anything works in our lives: God ordains that it should work. . . . *Whatever* God ordains to be will be, and *only* what he ordains to be will be. Difficult circumstances show us the reality of our lives: we are dependent on God for *absolutely everything*!"[1]

We can respond to trials in one of two ways: we can either look upward or we can look inward. But only one of those looks provides an accurate assessment of our situation and the help for which we yearn. If we turn inward for help, we will find ourselves devoid of comfort, because there are no answers to be found there. On the other hand, if we look up and out, we will see and believe God's good intentions toward us, and we will find ourselves increasingly able to live contentedly in times of trouble.

---

[1]Wayne Mack, *Humility: The Forgotten Virtue* (Phillipsburg, NJ: P&R, 2005), 128. Emphasis in original.

Triumph in Trials

Count it all joy, my brothers, when you meet trials of various kinds, for you know that the testing of your faith produces steadfastness. And let steadfastness have its full effect, that you may be perfect and complete, lacking in nothing.

JAMES 1:2–4

*S*usan puts her coffee cup in the sink with a sigh and goes to get the laundry started. Her heart is heavy as she sorts the clothes, thinking back on the strained conversation earlier that morning around the breakfast table. Her daughter Cassie had pushed away her cereal with a hard and angry face when denied permission to stay out past curfew on prom night. And Jim was no help, hiding behind his newspaper, letting her be the bad parent again. After Cassie left for school with a loud door slam, Susan tried to share her concerns about their daughter with Jim, but he cut her off with impatience. "She's sixteen," he said, turning his back and walking out of the kitchen. "Just let her be. She's miserable because you hover over her all the time." Susan just feels lonely day in and day out.

What aspects of day-to-day life do you find difficult to deal with? The answer is a little bit different for each of us, yet we all face issues and situations that threaten to push us into discouragement or depression. Perhaps there is a difficult relationship in your life that God isn't fixing. Or maybe you are perplexed about an unexpected direction your life has taken. Perhaps unanswered prayer is pressing you down; the longer you pray with no answer on the horizon, the farther away God seems. Whatever comes to mind in answer to these questions is a test—a wilderness, a weakness, or a trial—designed especially for you by a good God.

But we question his good intentions toward us and sink down in doubt and discouragement. "How can a kind God allow this?" we ask. "I'd never put my child through what God is doing to me." But God is a wiser parent than we could ever be. He places us in situations that provoke us, not to cause us to doubt but to strengthen us against our doubts. As someone wisely stated, "God may hurt you, but he will never harm you." And since that is true, we can—and must—be hope-filled:

> The danger at this point is to say something like, "Well, I have lost that something which I had, and obviously I shall not get it back again. But I am going on, and out of loyalty I will go on, as a sheer duty. . . . I will resign myself to my fate, I won't be a quitter, I won't turn my back on it, I will go on, though I go on feeling rather hopeless about it all." . . . That is the spirit of resignation, stoicism. Indeed I say that it is a temptation of the devil. If he can get God's people to lose hope, he will be content indeed.[1]

---

[1]D. Martyn Lloyd-Jones, *Spiritual Depression: Its Causes and Its Cures* (Grand Rapids, MI: Eerdmans, 1965), 194–195.

Destructive Desire

Let no one say when he is tempted,
"I am being tempted by God," for God cannot be
tempted with evil, and he himself tempts no one.
But each person is tempted when he is lured
and enticed by his own desire.

JAMES 1:13–14

Just two weeks earlier Joshua, their firstborn, had turned three. They'd held a little birthday celebration in honor of the occasion, but Joshua hadn't wanted his cake and ice cream. His tummy hurt, he had said, so Rachel made an appointment with the pediatrician. It all happened so fast after that; Rachel has trouble remembering the details. How had they gone from cake and candles to IV tubes and a hospital bed in just two short weeks? The slide from a tender tummy to life-threatening pain had taken only hours. But Rachel's pain is as great as Joshua's. Her child's suffering, not only from his illness but from all the tests and treatments, is torture for both of them. She can do nothing but hold his hand and fight off the agony of her helplessness to alleviate his suffering when he cries out to her to do so. "Why is God doing this?" Rachel wonders. "I'd do anything to take away his suffering. Why won't God do so if he is really able and really good?"

Suffering—ours and that of the people we love—so easily tempts us to doubt God's goodness. We want to trust him, but the horrible pain we are experiencing seems to prevent us from doing so. We tend to measure God by our own standards. We want ease, comfort, and minimal pain—for ourselves and perhaps even more for our loved ones. It just makes sense, doesn't it? If we would abolish in a heartbeat the pain experienced by those we love, it stands to reason that a God of love would do the same thing. If God has the power to intervene and the love to care but doesn't appear to act in keeping with those traits, it just seems logical to conclude that he is not as kind and good as we are.

The truth is, however, that God does want the best for us—the greatest happiness, joy, and comfort—but his ways for how we obtain them are very different from our ways. We simply lack the frame of reference that he has to see the big picture—the eternal picture. But even though we cannot see it, we can believe it. We won't be delivered from all our suffering in this lifetime, a fact that will keep us locked in fear if we keep our eyes on nothing but immediate relief. Peace comes when we see by faith what the apostle John saw in his vision: "He will wipe away every tear from their eyes, and death shall be no more, neither shall there be mourning, nor crying, nor pain anymore, for the former things have passed away" (Rev. 21:4).

Great Expectations

*He delivers the afflicted by their affliction
and opens their ear by adversity.*

JOB 36:15

*J*ob was a prosperous landowner who lived in ancient Israel, a wealthy man devoted to God. There came a point, however, when Job's entire life fell apart. He lost his livestock, and with it went his prosperity. Then all ten of his children were killed at one time. Despite his great grief, Job responded in faith. He said, "The LORD gave, and the LORD has taken away; blessed be the name of the LORD" (1:21). Job's sufferings weren't over yet though. God allowed him to be afflicted with painful sores all over his body, a condition so horrible that he could do nothing except sit in a heap. Added to this was the fact that his wife made it clear that she'd be well rid of Job when she told him, "Curse God and die" (2:9). While Job submitted to God during this painful season, his wife refused to do so.

We respond more like Job's wife than we do like Job most of the time, don't we? Ongoing trials tempt us to turn away from God because at some level we have an expectation that God's quota for testing us has been sufficiently filled for a season. "God," we say, "this has been hard. So I'm sure that's it for a while. Now I'm looking to see what sort of blessing you'll bring to compensate me for the pain." When a crisis hits, we initially cling to God with trust and hope. But what happens when things go from bad to worse? We start to fret because we think God isn't being fair. We put God in the dock, as C. S. Lewis said. We put him on trial, with ourselves as the prosecutors. But we are the ones in the wrong. The Bible never says that a bad patch inevitably will be followed by a good one, in this life anyway.

God is indeed good, and he is delighted when we cling to hopeful expectation for what he'll do in our difficulties. He is pleased when we trust in his love for us, a love that takes pleasure in delivering us from pain and heartache. But this sort of trust is very different from imposing onto him our idea of how things will be. To our way of thinking, our expectation is the "right" thing and therefore surely the thing that God will do for us. But often it is not. God's plans for our good are often radically different from our plans. Real trust isn't believing that God will do things as we expect he should; it is, rather, believing that whatever he does is good and perfect. We will only find relief from fear if we relinquish our expectations of what we think God ought to do for us and ask him to create within our hearts a trusting expectation for what he wills to do. If we are willing, we will find that his ways are far better than anything we could have chosen for ourselves.

A Broad Place

He delivers the afflicted by their affliction
and opens their ear by adversity.

JOB 36:15

*J*ob's three friends had been miserable comforters. In fact, they'd helped Job straight down the path of doubt and discouragement. But a fourth friend came to Job in the midst of his misery, and this man hit the nail on the head when he said, "Indeed He would have brought you out of dire distress, into a broad place where there is no restraint; and what is set on your table would be full of richness. But you are filled with the judgment due the wicked; judgment and justice take hold of you. . . . Take heed, do not turn to iniquity, for you have chosen this rather than affliction" (Job 36:16–21 NKJV).

What an eye-opener! God wanted to lift Job out of his misery, but Job had settled himself into his personal interpretation of the situation and refused to believe. His friend pointed out that Job was actually choosing his sin—his doubt and unbelief—rather than choosing submission to God's way, if God's way entailed suffering. Job chose to doubt, which kept him tied up in "dire distress." Unbelief and doubt about God will always make us afraid because when we are filled with doubt, we can't see that God is kind, loving, gracious, wise in all his ways toward us, and yearning to relate. As with our fears, Job's fears were actually the fruit of his own choosing.

Do we see ourselves in Job's predicament? Do we realize that we have a choice whether or not to be afraid? By refusing to accept his suffering, Job was refusing to trust God, which led to all his fear. Fear doesn't feel much like a choice. We'd do anything to be rid of it. Anything, that is, except submit to God if submission might mean pain or the loss of something we cherish. But when we are willing, when we make a choice to trust, we will find that our fear of pain and loss is far worse than the actual occurrence.

Going God's Way

All the paths of the LORD are steadfast love and faithfulness,
for those who keep his covenant and his testimonies.

P SALM 25:10

The prophet Jonah was a man whose mistrust of God led him to a horribly frightening place. God called Jonah to a particular path, a path that required him to go to the city of Nineveh and preach a message of repentance to the residents of that wicked city. But Jonah didn't think that was a good idea; so he ran away from God's call and ended up in the belly of a fish, a situation so awful that we cannot imagine his terror. Yet God used this scary place to teach Jonah a valuable truth: "Those who cling to worthless idols forfeit the grace that could be theirs" (Jon. 2:8 NIV).

What worthless idol did Jonah cling to that led him to turn away from God's grace and lovingkindness? Jonah hung on tightly to his right to determine what he wanted to do with his life, and what he wanted to do was just about anything other than see the wicked Ninevites saved. God let him go his own way, as he does with us when we insist on running our own show; but because God is merciful, he will make sure that any way we take away from him doesn't work out so well. At the same time, God didn't leave Jonah to get himself out of the mess he'd made of things. "The heart of man plans his way, but the LORD establishes his steps" (Prov. 16:9). God had plans for Jonah, and to be sure Jonah wouldn't miss out on them, he brought about a calamity designed to change Jonah's heart.

A big fish with an even bigger appetite accomplished God's purpose. Through a chaotic chain of events, Jonah found himself inside that great fish—a situation he just couldn't run from this time. Have you ever been cornered like Jonah? If so, you may recall the despair, the loss of all hope, and especially the misery of knowing that you were there because of your own doing. Perhaps that's where you are right now, in the belly of a fish that swallowed you in the midst of your own folly, and there is just no way out. But there really is a way out, and you will find it if, rather than sinking down in fear, you do what Jonah did: "When my life was fainting away, I remembered the LORD" (Jon. 2:7).

God doesn't leave us to clean up our messes. He steps in to help us find the path home. A wise pastor once said that God always breaks those whom he plans to use. Are you being broken right now? If so, cry out to God. He will meet you there and deliver you.

Peace in Hardship

*By faith Moses, when he was grown up, refused to be called
the son of Pharaoh's daughter, choosing rather to be
mistreated with the people of God than to enjoy
the fleeting pleasures of sin.*

Hebrews 11:24–25

*M*oses had reached a crossroads in his life, and he had
a very difficult choice to make. One road—remaining as a
member of the Egyptian royal family—was the road along
which he'd been traveling for most of his life. That was certainly the easier choice in many respects. As the grandson of
Pharaoh, Moses' position in society would have ensured him
great riches and personal power, security and privileged protection, the best foods, and the choicest women. But Moses
chose the other path, one that would, from the very moment
of his decision, eradicate every one of those privileges, many
of which he had enjoyed from his youth. Moses chose to walk
God's path with God's people. Moses' choice was a choice
to suffer.

How was Moses able to make such a choice? Walking
headlong into life-threatening difficulty goes against all
of our logic, doesn't it? We are fearful of suffering simply
overtaking us; where is the sanity in knowingly making a

choice to embrace it? Moses must have known that there was something—something overwhelmingly delightful—to be found along the path he chose that was enough to overpower his fears and misgivings. Moses was able to walk headlong into hardship without fear because it was the path of fellowship with God and God's people, blessings that provided him with more enjoyment than anything he would have found in Pharaoh's household. Moses also knew that a choice for God was a choice for superior protection. We find ourselves fearful much of the time because we are seeking safety in our jobs, our relationships, our homes, or our reputations. Real protection comes only from God, and we will find no lasting sense of safety anywhere else.

Moses didn't hem and haw about his choice either. When faced with a choice between suffering or creature comfort, Moses made a concrete decision. He didn't bargain with God, praying something like this: "Okay, God, I'll trust you up to a point, but if the price gets too high, well, that's a different story." Nor did he say, "If you were really good, Lord, you wouldn't put me into a dilemma like this." Sometimes we are called to make a faith choice that contradicts our reason. God's way appears scary; it seems as if there will be nothing but loss for us if we choose it. But if it's God's way, it's the best way, so we have nothing to fear. In fact, the only thing to fear is choosing the alternative. We can choose the right alternative the same way Moses did: "He considered the reproach of Christ greater wealth than the treasures of Egypt, for he was looking to the reward" (Heb. 11:26).

Remembering

"Is not this great Babylon, which I have built
by my mighty power as a royal residence and
for the glory of my majesty?"

DANIEL 4:30

*D*uring a dark period in the history of God's people, the Israelites were exiled from their homeland and forced to live in Babylon under the authority of the arrogant King Nebuchadnezzar. One of the Israelites who had to live in Babylon during this time was a prophet named Daniel. Nebuchadnezzar liked Daniel, and he elevated the young prophet to a high position in his court. As a result, Daniel was in a position to observe Nebuchadnezzar up close, and because of this we have some inside information on God's dealings with the egotistical king.

From Daniel we learn that Nebuchadnezzar wasn't that much different from you and me. At a time when Nebuchadnezzar was feeling pretty good about life, he took stock of his accomplishments and of the things he had acquired, and he attributed all his blessings to his own abilities. Don't we fall into the same delusion from time to time? We may not credit ourselves with the creation of an economic and military superpower such as ancient Babylon, but how often do we claim, "If I don't get the job done, who will?" or "It's up to me to make sure that this problem gets solved" or "I have to manage every detail of this project because I just don't trust that it will get done right any other way."

Thinking that our input or actions are necessary for success soon leads to the anxious, fearful, and inwardly focused belief that our world will fall apart if we don't hold it all together. We call it control. "Oh," we laugh, "I know I have control issues." Living as we do in a society that makes control a virtue, it's hard to recognize that such control is really a synonym for pride. Ugly and destructive attitudes such as pride are often hidden under a pretty mask, but our fear of losing control lets a bit of the ugliness peek through. How do we turn away from our compulsion to control and from the pride and anxiety that will always accompany it? We turn away by remembering.

> "*Beware lest you say in your heart, 'My power and the might of my hand have gotten me this wealth.' You shall remember the* LORD *your God, for it is he who gives you power to get wealth, that he may confirm his covenant that he swore to your fathers, as it is this day.*" (Deut. 8:17–18)

The Insanity of Unbelief

*At the end of the days I, Nebuchadnezzar, lifted my eyes
to heaven, and my reason returned to me, and I blessed the
Most High, and praised and honored him who lives forever,
for his dominion is an everlasting dominion, and his
kingdom endures from generation to generation.*

DANIEL 4:34

*N*ebuchadnezzar, king of Babylon, had a warped self-image—he thought too highly of himself. And like all who hold a grandiose self-view, he thought very little of God. Nebuchadnezzar isn't exactly the Bible character we want to be likened to, but chances are good that we reflect him more than we imagine we do. We just don't see it. But God sees it, and he knows that our warped self-image is because we have a warped image of him. Whenever we trust in ourselves rather than in God, we are acting like Nebuchadnezzar. "We've worked hard for this four-bedroom house in a quiet neighborhood, this community with a good school system for our kids, and our membership at the tennis club" may not be that different from Nebuchadnezzar's words, "Is not this great Babylon, which I have built by my mighty power as a royal residence and for the glory of my majesty?" (Dan.

4:30). This is sin. It is pride. It is insanity, as Nebuchadnezzar was about to find out.

God wants to correct our view both of him and of ourselves, and that's exactly what he did for Nebuchadnezzar. God set him free from his prideful delusion by demonstrating to Nebuchadnezzar who was really running the show in Babylon. God began by allowing Nebuchadnezzar to experience a taste of insanity:

> "O King Nebuchadnezzar, to you it is spoken: The kingdom has departed from you, and you shall be driven from among men, and your dwelling shall be with the beasts of the field. And you shall be made to eat grass like an ox, and seven periods of time shall pass over you, until you know that the Most High rules the kingdom of men and gives it to whom he will." Immediately the word was fulfilled against Nebuchadnezzar. He was driven from among men and ate grass like an ox, and his body was wet with the dew of heaven till his hair grew as long as eagles' feathers, and his nails were like birds' claws. (Dan. 4:31–33)

That was the most fitting thing God could do because insanity characterizes everyone who believes they can run their lives without God. What restored Nebuchadnezzar to a sane mind-set? The Bible is clear—Nebuchadnezzar looked up:

> At the end of the days I, Nebuchadnezzar, lifted my eyes to heaven, and my reason returned to me, and I blessed the Most High, and praised and honored him who lives forever. (v. 34)

Nebuchadnezzar's look upward was an act of humility, the acknowledgment that God is the One in control, and when the king was humbled, his reason—his sanity—was restored. One of the many evil fruits of self-reliance is the warping, the twisting, of how we see ourselves in relation to God. The bigger we allow ourselves to be, the smaller God becomes to us. We lose the ability to see that there are no real answers to be found within ourselves; we are broken, lost, and incapable of running our own lives. Is it any wonder that those of us with control issues live with chronic anxiety?

Nebuchadnezzar's thinking did a complete turnaround once his eyes were directed up to God and away from himself. His sanity returned, and he saw clearly that God "does according to his will among the host of heaven and among the inhabitants of the earth; and none can stay his hand or say to him, 'What have you done?'" (vv. 35–36). Nebuchadnezzar learned what we can learn too—there is no need to claim control when God has all the power and provision.

The Path to Healing

Naaman, commander of the army of the king of Syria,
was a great man with his master and in high favor,
because by him the LORD had given victory to Syria.
He was a mighty man of valor, but he was a leper."

2 KINGS 5:1

*C*ommander Naaman felt pretty good about himself, except for the fact that he had leprosy. Naaman was a successful warrior, and for that reason the king of Syria valued him and wanted him made well. So the king sent Naaman to the mighty Elisha, the prophet of Israel, to be healed. When Naaman appeared before Elisha, the prophet told him to go bathe in the Jordan River seven times. But rather than doing what Elisha instructed, Naaman became furious. Elisha's instructions didn't meet with Naaman's expectations. After all, couldn't a mighty warrior expect a healing with some fanfare and bells and whistles? Naaman had been telling himself, "He will surely come out to me, and stand and call on the name of the LORD his God, and wave his hand over the place, and heal the leprosy" (v. 11 NKJV). But that's not what Elisha did; he told Naaman simply to go dip in the river. The mighty warrior was greatly insulted.

What Naaman didn't know was that God intended the leprosy not to harm him but to humble him so that God could do him good. Naaman fretted a bit, but he wanted to be healed. So when his servants came and asked him, "If the prophet had told you to do something great, would you not have done it? How much more then, when he says to you, 'Wash, and be clean'?" (v. 13 NKJV), he was ready to listen. His servants brought to light what was keeping Naaman from the thing he most wanted—a desirble answer in his own way. But because Naaman wanted healing very badly, he swallowed his pride and did what Elisha had instructed. Naaman chose to go God's way, a path that ran contrary to his sense of reason and the way in which he thought things should be done, but it was the only path to his heart's desire.

Are we like Naaman? Are we locked onto a particular type of healing or blessing that we want God to do for us? Something we think God *should* do for us? If so, we may be unable to see the direction in which the blessing lies. It may seem that your employment problem is the thing that needs immediate healing, or those up-and-down mood swings, or the need to measure up to something or someone, or gaining control over an out-of-control relationship. But that very thing you want God to fix may be his instrument to teach you first to depend on him rather than on yourself or on peaceful circumstances.

The Bible says, "This is the way," but every fear-filled corner of our mind says, "No, that makes no sense." God says, "Trust me." We say, "Lord, I want to, but I can't because this doesn't match up with what I expected you to do." If we are anxious and fearful because we think God has forgotten to be gracious to us, could the reason be that we won't let go of our preconceived ideas of how things should go? Going God's way is an act of humility; it is also the only way where we will find a real solution to our problem.

The Weapons of Our Warfare

The weapons of our warfare are not of the flesh but have
divine power to destroy strongholds. We destroy arguments
and every lofty opinion raised against the knowledge of God,
and take every thought captive to obey Christ.

2 CORINTHIANS 10:4-5

Popular fiction depicting spiritual warfare has left a good number of fearful readers in its wake. The books on store shelves in recent years have made Satan big, God small, and evangelicals the determiners of the outcome. The stories claim to be based on Scripture, but most of them come from faulty interpretation. We don't have to be scared of Satan; in fact, it grieves God when we allow fears of the devil to rule our hearts. Besides, he is a defeated foe; Christ rendered him an all-time loser. "Resist the devil, and he will flee from you," says the apostle James (James 4:7).

We aren't called to fight the devil—we are called to resist him. We resist by refusing to listen to him. We don't have to sink down in discouragement when he plants the suggestion that our sins are too big to be forgiven, or when he whispers that God isn't the loving Father the Bible says he is, or when he tempts us to believe that the lust of the flesh, the lust of the eyes, and the pride of life are more desirable than God's

ways. We resist him not by mastering offensive techniques of
spiritual warfare, as some think, or by rebuking him directly.
It is the Lord who rebukes Satan (see Zech. 3:2; Jude 9).

We also resist the devil by putting on the whole armor of
God (see Eph. 6:10–18). We fight by believing the truth of
God's Word, walking in paths of righteousness, reminding
ourselves of the gospel message and carrying it to others,
exercising our faith, and praying constantly. We resist the
devil by trusting in God's fatherly love toward us in Christ
instead of trusting our feelings and our attempts to earn
God's favor.

As we give Christ more room in our hearts and minds
and affections, the devil loses his foothold. Don't be afraid,
because even when you are weak in God's ways, Christ
is strong on your behalf, and he will hold you up. He has
already defeated the devil for you.

Getting Personal

"Hagar, Sarai's maid, where have you come from,
and where are you going?"

*H*agar, maidservant to Abraham's wife, Sarah, knew firsthand about fear. Servants in ancient Israel had few options in terms of jobs and lifestyle; so when unpleasant working conditions arose, servants often had little choice but to endure them. Hagar found herself in just such a predicament.

God had promised to bring Sarah and Abraham a child, but after years of waiting, the couple decided to take matters into their own hands and obtain a child through a surrogate, and they chose Hagar. It worked, but soon thereafter Sarah became jealous of Hagar and her pregnancy and began to abuse her. The situation became bad enough to incite Hagar to run away into the wilderness to escape the mistreatment. It was there in the wilderness that the angel of the Lord found her and told her to return to Sarah, which she did, calling "the name of the LORD who spoke to her, 'You are a God of seeing,' for she said, 'Truly here I have seen him who looks after me'" (Gen. 16:13).

Later, after her baby, Ishmael, was born, Hagar wound

up back in the wilderness, her infant son along with her, although this time she had not run away—she had been banished by the jealous Sarah. She was terrified. She and the child were out of water, so she placed Ishmael under a shrub to die. "Then she went and sat down opposite him a good way off . . . for she said, 'Let me not look on the death of the child.' And as she sat opposite him, she lifted up her voice and wept" (Gen. 21:16). But once again God met her and assured her of his promises, protection, and provision: "What troubles you, Hagar? Fear not, for God has heard the voice of the boy where he is. Up! Lift up the boy, and hold him fast with your hand, for I will make him into a great nation" (vv. 17–18).

God met Hagar in a place of isolation, deprivation, and fear. It was there, in the midst of bleak circumstances, that she received guidance and comfort in a very personal way. If you read through the entire story of Hagar, Abraham, and Sarah, you will see that the angel of the Lord is the only one who calls Hagar by name.

God often brings us into the wilderness, too, for the same reasons. He wants to get personal with us, and sometimes it takes a wilderness to make us open to hearing him and to receiving his instruction. Are you in a wilderness? No matter how you got there, God's sovereign hand has guided every step. Rather than looking at your dark and fearful circumstances, look for him and you will discover that he is right there, ready to lead you forward.

Fickle Hearts

"Would that we had died by the hand of the LORD
*in the land of Egypt, when we sat by the meat pots and
ate bread to the full, for you have brought us out into
this wilderness to kill this whole assembly with hunger."*

EXODUS 16:3

*M*iraculous deliverance! God had parted the waters of
the sea, rescuing his people from the hands of Pharaoh. The
Israelites praised God, singing, "The LORD is my strength
and my song, and he has become my salvation; this is my
God, and I will praise him, my father's God, and I will exalt
him" (Exod. 15:2).

However, just two months and sixteen days later,
the Israelites had come to think of God as their enemy.
Wildernesses are barren places, and when God leads us into
one—a circumstance where we struggle to find even our
daily necessities—it is hard to detect his good hand in the
experience. Nevertheless, God is there, as he always is, and
this truth must be believed by faith when we cannot perceive
it by sight.

The Israelites fell into despair and fear because doubt
skewed their perspective and made their circumstances
appear overwhelming and impossible. They stopped believ-

ing that the God who had led them out of one difficult place would surely not fail them in another. When they had lacked food, God had provided manna. When they had been unsure of their way forward, God had led them with a pillar of cloud by day and a pillar of fire by night. In fact he provided them with fellowship, leadership, food, rest, and protection during every year of their wilderness wandering.

Perhaps you are living in a wilderness right now—a mile-high communication barrier between you and your husband, or a teenaged daughter who seems to hate you, or a dead-end job with no hope on the horizon, or a yearning to be married with no prospect in sight. Rest assured that whatever may have brought you into this wilderness, God has been behind it all. He knows exactly what he wants to accomplish in you and in the others involved, and it is something that could not be done in any other way. And since it is ultimately God who has brought you into the wilderness, he will surely provide for you there, and in his own perfect time and way he will bring you out.

Warped Perceptions

And the LORD said to Moses, "How long will this people despise me? And how long will they not believe in me, in spite of all the signs that I have done among them?"

NUMBERS 14:11

As the Israelites neared the end of their long sojourn in the wilderness, the Promised Land lay just before them. God instructed Moses to send spies to investigate Canaan, the bountiful land of promise. Would the food be good? Would the natives of Canaan be fierce and cruel? Would the land be sufficiently fruitful to enable a permanent settlement for a nation the size of Israel? The spies went forth, and when they returned, the news they brought wasn't good. They claimed, "We are not able to go up against the people, for they are stronger than we are" (Num. 13:31). Can you see their problem? God had promised to give this land into their hands, a land flowing with milk and honey, but rather than take God at his word, they just looked at the difficulties. Rather than doubt their own viewpoint, they doubted God's.

Sometimes we are tempted to think that we cannot help our unbelief; we excuse it because we can't see any possible solution to our troubles. But the Bible doesn't support that. God blamed the Israelites for their unbelief, not the intensity of their troubles. Refusing to trust God is actually to "despise God," as God himself made clear to Moses. How we hurt him by our mistrust!

God had great blessing in store for the Israelites, if only they would trust him. The writer of Hebrews wrote, "Therefore, as the Holy Spirit says, 'Today, if you hear his voice, do not harden your hearts as in the rebellion, on the day of testing in the wilderness, where your fathers put me to the test and saw my works for forty years. Therefore I was provoked with that generation, and said, "They always go astray in their heart; they have not known my ways." As I swore in my wrath, "They shall not enter my rest."'" (Heb. 3:7–11).

Let's not be like the Israelites who missed out on great blessing because they refused to trust the Lord. We can enter into God's rest only if we take him at his word. Are you facing an insurmountable obstacle today, something bringing you to the brink of despair? Quit looking at your inability. Nothing is impossible with God, and you will find a clear path ahead if you look at him instead.

A Divine Feast

*"And you shall remember the whole way that the
LORD your God has led you these forty years in
the wilderness, that he might humble you, testing you
to know what was in your heart, whether you would
keep his commandments or not. And he humbled you
and let you hunger and fed you with manna, which you
did not know, nor did your fathers know, that he might
make you know that man does not live by bread alone,
but man lives by every word that comes from the
mouth of the LORD."*

DEUTERONOMY 8:2-3

*C*harlotte has wanted a baby ever since she got married
six years ago. Her hopes have been raised with each pregnancy, only to have them dashed to pieces as soon as the
telltale signs begin. Three pregnancies. Three miscarriages.
No baby. Charlotte is heavy-hearted much of the time, and
very perplexed. God seems so distant; she can't find his comfort. But Charlotte goes through the motions, getting up each
morning to read her Bible and to pray, attending Bible study
and worship each week with her husband, and making a nice

home. What else can she do? Her desire remains constant even as her hopes diminish.

What is God up to in Charlotte's life? Trials such as Charlotte's, the kind from which there is no escape in front or behind, the kind that are not bad enough to make us want to stop living but cover all we do with a black cloud, just go on and on with no relief in sight. Why does God do this to those he loves? It just makes no sense to our way of thinking.

We don't know all the reasons, but one thing we do know is that God is teaching Charlotte that he is adequate for all her needs. She doesn't actually need a baby; she just needs Jesus. Only God can make Christ and his lordship her first priority, her greatest desire, and he is actually doing it for her in and through her pain. And she may get her baby yet.

Are you living in the wilderness right now? God may never reveal to you the specific reason for your suffering, but he will always show you what you really need. Remember Job? He came out of his wilderness experience with deeper faith and with a double portion of all he had lost. But before he got there, he made a decision to cling to God in the midst of his pain. While still in the wilderness Job stopped questioning God's goodness and simply considered his character. As a result, even before his losses were restored to him, Job was able to cry out, "I know that you can do all things, and that no purpose of yours can be thwarted" (Job 42:2).

Will you trust in God's sovereign goodness right now, today, even before you know the outcome of your trouble? If so, here is what you can expect: "We consider those blessed who remained steadfast. You have heard of the steadfastness of Job, and you have seen the purpose of the Lord, how the Lord is compassionate and merciful" (James 5:11).

A Haven from Heartbreak

O God, you are my God; earnestly I seek you;
my soul thirsts for you; my flesh faints for you,
as in a dry and weary land where there is no water.

Psalm 63:1

King David spent a good bit of time in the wilderness fleeing for his life, both before and after becoming king. The wilderness was a good place to hide from those who sought to kill him. But safety wasn't his greatest concern; it was also a time of great pain for David since those who wanted to kill him were family members. Before David became king, his father-in-law, Saul, was king of Israel, and he wanted David out of the picture. Saul was jealous of David and felt threatened by David's strength and integrity. But the greatest pain of all for David came years later when his son Absalom wanted to steal his throne and sought to do so by murdering him.

It doesn't get more horrible than that—fleeing into the wilderness because your own son is trying to kill you. David certainly understood the pain of relational betrayal. But in the midst of his loss of love on a human level, David found a deeper, more reliable love in his God: "Because your steadfast love is better than life, my lips will praise you. So I will bless you as long as I live; in your name I will lift up my hands. My soul will be satisfied as with fat and rich food, and my mouth will praise you with joyful lips" (Ps. 63:3–5).

How could David find satisfaction when members of his family were seeking to kill him? We can't even imagine. But if David found relief and joy in the middle of such utter betrayal, we can too. God will be all for us that we allow him to be. That bears repeating: God will be all for us that we allow him to be. So rather than sinking down in fear or giving in to self-pity or demanding an explanation for our suffering, we can turn to God in faith and find his love more satisfying than the love of another person. No matter who betrays us, God never will. God's love is the only love that will never let us down.

A Woman's Wilderness

*"Therefore, behold, I will allure her, and bring her into
the wilderness, and speak tenderly to her. And there
I will give her her vineyards and make the Valley of Achor
a door of hope. And there she shall answer as in the days of
her youth, as at the time when she came out of the land
of Egypt. And in that day, declares the* LORD,
*you will call me 'My Husband,' and no longer
will you call me 'My Baal.'"*

HOSEA 2:14–16

*G*omer was a pleasure-seeker, a woman who placed her
needs and wants ahead of everything and everyone in her life.
She was married to the Old Testament prophet Hosea, but
Hosea wasn't meeting her needs quite the way she wished. So
Gomer took a lover, and then another, and then another. Her
life went downhill with each new affair. What started out as
fun and games quickly became empty and hard, which is the
way sin always works. But Gomer's husband, Hosea, had
never stopped loving her, and he went to great lengths to get
her back. Why did Hosea bother with his cheating wife? He
persevered out of obedience to God, who told him to take
her back. Hosea's marriage became his ministry—a living

sermon about how God's people were committing adultery against God.

We read Gomer's story and think, "I'd never do that!" But our anxious quests for self-satisfaction, our self-reliant schemes for happiness that leave Christ out, are acts of spiritual adultery. We aren't all that different from Gomer much of the time. But just as Hosea went to great lengths to get his wife back, God does that with us when we stray from him.

Perhaps you are in that very place today. Maybe you've wandered away from God in an attempt to fill a lonely place in your heart or to stop the clamor of a strong craving, and you find yourself miserable and afraid of the consequences from this predicament of your own making. But consider what God is saying to you through the prophet Hosea. God has brought you into a wilderness not to punish you but to meet you—right where your sin has taken you—with his love and mercy and to bring you home. Jesus Christ is your loving and kind Lord; he loves you with a jealous love, and he will never let you go.

The Wonder of Weakness

And Jacob was left alone. And a man wrestled with him until the breaking of the day. When the man saw that he did not prevail against Jacob, he touched his hip socket, and Jacob's hip was put out of joint as he wrestled with him. Then he said, "Let me go, for the day has broken." But Jacob said, "I will not let you go unless you bless me."

GENESIS 32:24–26

*E*motional, physical, spiritual, or intellectual—all weakness is scary. Weakness makes us feel out of control and unable to manage our lives. But weakness is actually a blessing in disguise.

The patriarch Jacob discovered this one night in the desert. Jacob was a man used to getting ahead in life by tricking others; he wasn't the most upstanding man in ancient Israel. Jacob manipulated people and circumstances because he feared what would happen to him if he didn't. But the truth is that his dishonest dealings were the direct result of his failure to trust God to provide for him.

Jacob's chicanery caught up with him one night in the desert, a place to which he'd fled after tricking his father-in-law in a business deal. Jacob was fleeing to his homeland—a wise move under the circumstances. However, on the way home Jacob was about to come face-to-face with his brother, Esau, from whom he had stolen something years before. And Jacob, reaping the results of sowing at another's expense, was anxious about how the meeting would go. On the road behind him was his angry father-in-law, Laban, and on the path ahead was the offended Esau with a vast number of supporters in tow. Jacob was trapped, which was exactly where God wanted him. There, with no safe place to hide from the consequences of his character, an Angel came and wrestled with Jacob throughout the night. When Jacob refused to submit, the Angel put Jacob's hip out of joint in order to end the wrestling match. God had his way with Jacob, and although Jacob walked with a limp for the remainder of his life, he was a less fearful, more trusting man than ever before.

Do we see ourselves in Jacob? If we are not trusting God, we will find ourselves seeking what we want and the things we think we need in other ways, no matter what we have to do to get them. But God knows what we are doing. He knows how destructive such a lifestyle is for us and for those we misuse, and he is faithful to wrestle us away from our manipulative behavior. In fact, God will go to great lengths to free us from the cheap tricks we use to get what we want and the fear that inevitably comes when we try to live by our wits. Is God wrestling with you? If so, allow that hip to be displaced. You will find great blessing. Jacob did:

> *Esau ran to meet him and embraced him and fell on his neck and kissed him, and they wept. . . . Jacob said . . . "I have seen your face, which is like seeing the face of God, and you have accepted me. Please accept my blessing that is brought to you, because God has dealt graciously with me, and because I have enough" (Gen. 33:4, 10–11).*

Thorns of Blessing

*Three times I pleaded with the Lord about this,
that it should leave me. But he said to me,
"My grace is sufficient for you, for my power is made
perfect in weakness." Therefore I will boast all the more
gladly of my weaknesses, so that the power of Christ may
rest upon me. For the sake of Christ, then, I am content
with weaknesses, insults, hardships, persecutions,
and calamities. For when I am weak, then I am strong.*

2 Corinthians 12:8–10

A debilitating ailment hinders us from enjoying an active life . . . a shrinking income robs us of financial breathing room to pay the bills . . . an elderly in-law moves in, sucking the peace out of our home. Difficulties like these—frustrating, worrisome, stressful—happen to each one of us. Such difficulties may occur overnight; at other times they creep up on us over time.

Do you know what I'm talking about? Maybe you can relate from personal experience. Perhaps there is a difficult situation you are trying to cope with right now, something making you anxious and irritable much of the time. Surely you have prayed about it. Paul prayed several times about his personal problem, asking God to deliver him from his "thorn . . . in the flesh" (v. 7). But God did not deliver him in the way he asked. God gave him the strength of Christ instead.

Paul's thorn weakened him in some way, just as our difficulties weaken us. As we fight off the continual jabbing of the thorn, we seek to pray our way back to strength. But more often than not, the thorn we want gone is the very thing God is using to accomplish something good in us. Paul's weakened condition made room for the strength of Christ, a strength he would need for all that lay ahead, a strength that would give him a larger capacity to enjoy the blessings that God had in store for him. Weakness in God's people is always a blessing in disguise, but it's hard to see it as such when we are feeling it keenly. We look for any escape, any way we can find back to the strength of self-sufficiency and daily tranquillity.

While we are anxiously looking for a way out, what we don't see is that our thorn isn't our real problem. What is actually making us anxious is our heart's demand to be free of it. If we'd just stop resisting, we'd find grace to live peacefully with our difficult spouse, our multiple sclerosis, or our unemployment. If we are willing, we will find that we really don't need the thorn removed—divine grace is sufficient. God will prove that to us if we let him.

Sweet Rest

*"Come to me, all who labor and are heavy laden,
and I will give you rest. Take my yoke upon you, and
learn from me, for I am gentle and lowly in heart,
and you will find rest for your souls.
For my yoke is easy, and my burden is light."*

MATTHEW 11:28-30

Rest? Some of us don't get what Jesus was talking about here. For some of us, living the Christian life just feels like a burden. Prayer is a source of stress; how do we know if we are praying in the right way? And temptations are always there, pressing in everywhere we turn. There are so many things to remember and get right. Is this your view of life in God's kingdom? If so, it explains why Jesus' words here in Matthew make no sense to you. Of course, there is no rest for those of us who worry about getting it right all the time.

Prayer is not enjoyable if we think that God's hearing us is contingent upon how well we pray or how often, or on getting the phraseology just right. Anxiety about prayer robs us—and God—of the fellowship for which we have been redeemed. How do we break away from prayer pressure? We break away by recognizing that our prayers are not what change things, contrary to the popular bumper sticker. God is the one who changes things, which is why we do not need to worry about the perfection of our prayers. Paul wrote, "Likewise the Spirit helps us in our weakness. For we do not know what to pray for as we ought, but the Spirit himself intercedes for us with groanings too deep for words" (Rom. 8:26).

We are also weak in our ability to resist temptation, but this is another weight we do not have to carry alone. Scripture tells us, "No temptation has overtaken you that is not common to man. God is faithful, and he will not let you be tempted beyond your ability, but with the temptation he will also provide the way of escape, that you may be able to endure it" (1 Cor. 10:13).

Jesus Christ is filled with compassion concerning our struggles, "for we do not have a high priest who is unable to sympathize with our weaknesses, but one who in every respect has been tempted as we are, yet without sin. Let us then with confidence draw near to the throne of grace, that we may receive mercy and find grace to help in time of need" (Heb. 4:15–16).

Jesus is the only resting place. In fact, Jesus *is* rest. Lean on him, and walking with God will no longer feel burdensome. It will become your greatest delight.

The Choice Is Yours

Thus says the LORD:
"Cursed is the man who trusts in man
and makes flesh his strength,
whose heart turns away from the LORD.
He is like a shrub in the desert,
and shall not see any good come.
He shall dwell in the parched places of the wilderness,
in an uninhabited salt land."

JEREMIAH 17:5–6

$\mathcal{E}$rin has high expectations for her friendships. She gives a lot of her time and energy to those she cares about, and she expects the same in return. Although Erin's friends love her, many of them don't lean the same weight on the friendship as she does, and consequently Erin is anxious much of the time, steeling herself for the next relational letdown or disappointment.

Erin is experiencing the truth of Jeremiah's words. Perhaps you are too. The prophet actually declares that we are cursed if we entrust our hearts and lives into the hands of human beings. It's quite logical, really: since people are sinners, they are going to disappoint us. If we choose people as our safety, sooner or later our lives will become barren and unfruitful, like a shrub in the desert, a defenseless plant out of reach from anything that can nourish and sustain it. Choosing to trust someone unreservedly—a friend, our spouse, our child—with our security and well-being actually blinds us to blessings. Jeremiah makes clear that we will be unable to see when good comes. That's a frightening prospect. God has many good things in store for us, but if we are seeking our own means of fulfillment, our eyes aren't looking in his direction.

Jeremiah offers an alternative lifestyle—trusting in God instead. If we seek security in God, we will be like "a tree planted by water, that sends out its roots by the stream, and does not fear when heat comes, for its leaves remain green, and is not anxious in the year of drought, for it does not cease to bear fruit" (Jer. 17:7–8).

Are you trusting in God or are you looking to the people in your life to satisfy you? Only God really knows. Jeremiah concludes his botanical illustration with God's words: "The heart is deceitful above all things, and desperately sick; who can understand it? I the LORD search the heart and test the mind, to give every man according to his ways, according to the fruit of his deeds" (vv. 9–10). If, like Erin, you find your relationships unsatisfying and a constant source of stress, if you are frequently disappointed by the people in your life, if you feel more like a withering shrub than a flourishing tree, God knows the truth about it. Invite him into your heart—into first place—and you will find him to be everything you've wanted but have been unable to find.

Good in Every Way

I believe that I shall look upon the goodness of the LORD in the land of the living!

PSALM 27:13

*M*ost of the single women I have known over the years have desired to be married. They have prayed long and hard for God's provision of a mate, and surely many of those prayers were answered with godly marriages. Others have received a different sort of answer—grace to remain single with contentment and calls to amazing opportunities. Others seem not to have received any answer at all to that prayer. As the years go on, their discontentment lingers and their anxiety increases. Oh, they recognize God's blessings in their lives—great jobs, lots of friends, good churches—but they just can't get past the fear that their chances for having a family of their own are growing dimmer by the year. As a result, they do not enjoy their single years, nor are they able to serve God with joy in day-to-day things.

Perhaps you are struggling with your marital status. If not this, maybe there is something else going on, something in which you feel caught in the anxious limbo of life-on-hold until God brings along what you need. The reason we remain anxious and caught in unhappy limbo is not because we are lacking something we need—it is because we aren't trusting God. And the reason we aren't trusting him, although we may not recognize it, is because deep down in our hearts we don't really believe God is being good to us in allowing us to linger where we are. When struggles to trust God arise, it is always because at some level we don't really believe he is good.

God always has our best in mind, and he works to bring it about, no matter how it may look initially to our way of thinking. We can trust him. We can trust that the reason we are single today is because God is being good to us today. We can trust that we don't have a baby today, or a job, or good health, because God is being good to us. "The LORD is righteous in all his ways and kind in all his works. The LORD is near to all who call on him, to all who call on him in truth. He fulfills the desire of those who fear him; he also hears their cry and saves them" (Ps. 145:17–19).

Our Good Father

Bless the LORD, O my soul,
and all that is within me, bless his holy name!
Bless the LORD, O my soul,
and forget not all his benefits. . . .
As a father shows compassion to his children,
so the LORD shows compassion to those who fear him.

Psalm 103:1–2, 13

Beth did not have a good father growing up, the sort that other little girls had, a father who loved and protected them, provided for their needs, and hugged them when they were sad. Today, as an adult, Beth is mistrustful of God. Because the concept of fatherhood is painful for her, Beth has built a self-protective wall around her heart, but that hasn't made her feel safe and joyful. To the contrary, Beth is riddled with almost constant anxiety. She has listened too long to those who nod sympathetically and say, "Of course you struggle to trust God. It will take a lifetime to really let him into your heart." Such sympathy is actually harming Beth.

Did you grow up with a bad dad? Many women did. But that fact doesn't exclude them from experiencing and enjoying the perfect fatherhood of God. In fact, it may actually be a means for knowing his fatherhood in the deepest possible way. If you did not have a godly and good father, God will gladly provide you with good fathering from other sources, first and foremost from himself and often through others as well—pastors, teachers, friends, and perhaps a new family of your own. One way or another, good fathering is available to all of God's daughters because he is the only true father (Matt. 23:9).

Because God comes to us through Christ as a father, we can know beyond a shadow of a doubt that his will for us is to understand and experience good fathering. God wants you to know him as your real and eternal Father, one who knows you thoroughly and who yearns to fellowship with you. He is the sort of Father who knows what you need before you ask (Matt. 6:8) and a Father who freely forgives. He is a father who "forgives all your iniquity, who heals all your diseases, who redeems your life from the pit, who crowns you with steadfast love and mercy, who satisfies you with good" (Ps. 103:3–5). This is what your real Father is like. No matter what sort of father you had growing up, God is the Father you will have forever.

Your Place in God's Family

*For you did not receive the spirit of slavery to fall back
into fear, but you have received the Spirit of adoption as sons,
by whom we cry, "Abba! Father!" The Spirit himself
bears witness with our spirit that we are children of God,
and if children, then heirs—heirs of God and
fellow heirs with Christ, provided we suffer with him
in order that we may also be glorified with him.*

ROMANS 8:15-17

*G*od is our Father, and he sees each of us as his own
unique and precious child. How can we be sure? We know
because we've been given the Holy Spirit. We know because
we have a yearning for God in our soul. We know because we
care what God thinks, we care about whether we are rightly
related to him.

Doubts and fears are bound to assail us if we lack assurance that we are truly part of God's family or if we get
anxious about doing something that might jeopardize membership in this family. But the very fact that we even worry
about it can provide us the assurance we lack. Unbelievers
don't care about being right with God. In fact, they don't care
about God at all. "In the pride of his face the wicked does not

seek him; all his thoughts are, 'There is no God'" (Ps. 10:4). The very fact that we are anxious about pleasing God ought to quell the anxiety about our standing with him.

Our adopted status is official and can never be retracted. Jesus redeemed us and presented us to God the Father for all time. Before Jesus came to earth, men and women did not refer to God by the New Testament term *Abba*, a name for "father" signifying closeness and affection. Once Jesus came, all that changed. Jesus became the link between God the Father and his people. It is only in Christ that God becomes *Abba*; once we are united to Christ, our place as God's children is eternally secure. The apostle John wrote, "See what kind of love the Father has given to us, that we should be called children of God; and so we are" (1 John 3:1).

God loved you so much that he sacrificed his only Son to bring you close in order to fellowship with you. There is no greater joy, no greater privilege, than that of enjoying your heavenly Father. If you believe in the completed work of Christ for you, then God is your Father.

Where Is Your Faith?

*And a great windstorm arose, and the waves were
breaking into the boat, so that the boat was already filling.
But he was in the stern, asleep on the cushion.
And they woke him and said to him, "Teacher,
do you not care that we are perishing?" And he awoke
and rebuked the wind and said to the sea, "Peace! Be still!"
And the wind ceased, and there was a great calm.
He said to them, "Why are you so afraid?
Have you still no faith?"*

MARK 4:37–40

*W*hy are you so afraid?" Jesus asked his disciples. He
didn't ask in order to find the answer; he already knew the
answer. Jesus was exposing the unbelief that was the source
of their fear. Because Jesus was with them, they had nothing
to worry about. The same is true of us once we belong to him.
No trial, tragedy, or crisis can befall us without the protective
hand of Jesus covering us.

Do we really know the security we have in Christ? We
haven't realized it yet if things go wrong and we wonder what
we must do to get God to help us. We haven't quite understood what security in Christ is if we miss our quiet time one

morning and think we'll be thrown off course all day. We don't yet know our riches in Christ if we think we have to reach some spiritual peak before God will give us a husband or fix our marriage or save our children. We haven't quite grasped the true gospel if we are living in chronic worry, fear, or anxiety. "Come to me, all who labor and are heavy laden, and I will give you rest," Jesus says (Matt. 11:28). The rest that Jesus is talking about is our spiritual birthright in Christ. It's a rest that offers us peace, enrichment, wisdom, fearlessness, and purpose. Most of all, it brings us the quietness of heart for which we so desperately yearn, the awareness that we are safe, secure, and loved by our heavenly Father. No matter the storm whirling around us, we are safe in union with Christ Jesus.

Perhaps the waves are kicking up in your life today, and the wind is howling. Jesus has not left you. Although it may appear as if Jesus is asleep and unable to care for you, rest assured that he is in complete control of your life. He can calm your storm with a single word.

A Fence against Fear

Keep your heart with all vigilance, for from it flow the springs of life.

P R O V E R B S   4 : 2 3

*E*ve dialoged with the serpent, and she lost the battle (Gen. 3:1–6). "Now the serpent was more crafty than any other beast of the field that the LORD God had made. He said to the woman, 'Did God actually say . . . ?'" The battle was lost the moment Eve turned toward him with a listening ear and an open heart.

The devil is stronger and smarter than we are; so arguing with him won't help us very much and can actually enhance our difficulty. Jesus has provided us with the way to resist. When he was tempted by the devil in the wilderness, Jesus refuted him with Scripture (Matt. 4:1–11). Scripture is the offensive weapon in our arsenal for waging spiritual warfare. The apostle Paul called God's Word "the sword of the Spirit" (Eph. 6:17). When Satan assails you with accusations, you don't have to listen or respond to his lies. He may suggest that you are a substandard Christian or appeal to your senses with something illicit or tell you God isn't good, but there are Scripture passages to refute every one of his lies. Immersing ourselves in the Bible is one of the primary ways we keep, or guard, our hearts.

Sometimes the keeping of our hearts requires us to run away. "The name of the LORD is a strong tower; the righteous man runs into it and is safe" (Prov. 18:10). We must run to our "strong tower," to Christ, when we are tempted to believe anything that contradicts the truth of God's lovingkindness. We must run to him if we are faced with overwhelming temptation to sin. We must run to him when life is crashing down around us and we are questioning our faith.

We also guard our hearts by disciplining our minds. Our minds are the key place where spiritual battles are won or lost. We know this is true because we are promised peace as long as our minds are fixed on God: "You keep him in perfect peace whose mind is stayed on you, because he trusts in you" (Isa. 26:3). Paul said, "Set your mind on things that are above, not on things that are on earth. For you have died, and your life is hidden with Christ in God" (Col. 3:2–3). Paul also advises us to focus our thoughts on things that are true, honorable, just, pure, lovely, commendable, excellent, and praiseworthy (Phil. 4:8). Are our thoughts about God excellent and commendable, or are we failing to believe the best about him?

Guarding our hearts is the most practical thing we can do to prevent fear from closing in on us, and it is something we are well able to do because "God gave us a spirit not of fear but of power and love and self-control" (2 Tim. 1:7).

Are You Sure?

*Now there is in Jerusalem by the Sheep Gate a pool,
in Aramaic called Bethesda, which has
five roofed colonnades. In these lay a multitude of
invalids—blind, lame, and paralyzed.
One man was there who had been an invalid for
thirty-eight years. When Jesus saw him lying there and
knew that he had already been there a long time,
he said to him, "Do you want to be healed?"*

JOHN 5:2-6

*J*esus asked the crippled man, "Do you want to get well?"
Let's ask ourselves the same thing concerning our anxiety. Do
we want to be free of our fears? According to God's Word,
we can be free; we have a choice in the matter.

The man in the pool really did want to get well; so Jesus
healed him then and there. Right now, today, we have a
choice, one that we may have to make not once but every day
for the rest of our lives: we can cling either to our own way
of thinking and living, or we can cast our cares and ourselves
on Jesus Christ and on the all-powerful, all-loving, all-wise
heavenly Father. Will we choose to trust that God is utterly

sovereign over our lives and over everything that happens to us? If so, we will find him trustworthy.

Our Father loves us, and as we grasp more of the fullness of that love, our fears will evaporate. "There is no fear in love, but perfect love casts out fear. For fear has to do with punishment, and whoever fears has not been perfected in love" (1 John 4:18). The degree to which we believe that God loves us is the degree to which our fears will diminish.

We must choose to stop believing that our anxieties will all go away if only our circumstances would change. Included in our choice to get well is correctly identifying the real issue at the core of our fears, worries, and anxieties—our relationship with God. We must choose to pray for humble hearts that enable a clear view of God's kindness and love and power before we ask him to free us from daily chaos, relational disharmony, and any other messy aspect of our lives. God longs to lead us to the rest of soul that makes for joy, but we have a choice in the matter—the choice of joy and peace.